Plan 4 It:
The 4 Essential
Master Plans for
Every Church

Tim Cool

Plan 4 It: The 4 Essential Master Plans for Every Church
© 2015 by Tim Cool

Published by Rainer Publishing
www.rainerpublishing.com

ISBN 978-0692567289
Printed in the United States of America

CONTENTS

Introduction

Meet Pastor Bob. He is the pastor of First Church somewhere, anywhere, everywhere.

His church is not just non-denominational, but also Presbyterian, Baptist, Methodist, Episcopal, Anglican, Lutheran, Nazarene, Assembly of God, Charismatic, Independent, among others. In short, he is my pastor and your pastor. He is my father, who was a Wesleyan pastor for over twenty-five years. He represents any leader of a church or ministry who has or ever will consider a facilities expansion or building program. He is the embodiment of every person who has led a growing organization and who has felt a leading from the Lord to explore how physical facilities may serve as a tool to further the growth, influence, and ministry of the church.

I have spent the past 30 years working with "Bobs" and their teams to navigate the rough waters of facilities expansion projects across the United States. I worked with these ministries to navigate issues related to land and site selection, zoning and re-zoning, master planning, architectural review processes, schematic design coordination, construction document coordination, value engineering, generosity and financing, pre-construction, entitlements, construction management, post-construction, life cycle management, and just about everything in between. During that time I have been blessed to serve over 400 ministries, helping to explore and implement their facility needs and wants.

Many of these projects required significant prayer and soul-searching to determine the real needs and motivations behind such an endeavor. I have worked with many "Bobs" who have huge a vision—sometimes even unrealistic visions. But at least these pastors had a vision. In those cases we had to take the time to dive deep into the issues associated with the vision as well as the significant aspects of financial capability and practicality of the vision.

These processes were not always pleasant, but when the church was willing to invest the time, energy, and resources to work through them, the results were remarkable. Not only did I witness churches making the right choices for their situations, but I also saw hearts melted and visions set on fire by the passion and the coming together of God's people for a common purpose. This is what drives me, what keeps me up at night, and what makes me crazy at times.

My passion is not driven by conceiving plans, digging dirt, developing facilities, or maintaining completed structures. What I am passionate about is assisting churches, ministries, and their leadership to be intentional stewards of the things with which God has entrusted them—the people, communities, ministry opportunities, and of course, their facilities.

The master planning process is not merely a formal exercise to add more meetings to an already-busy church calendar; it is the foundation of any facility-related initiative. It is essential to every ministry in each of the four areas that we are going to discuss. Why do I say they are essential? Think about what essential means. It is best defined as "absolutely necessary; extremely important." Planning is not just a good idea or something that we might get a-round-to-it. It is essential.

As most of you know, I am not a theologian and I did not go to seminary, but I am confident the Bible is clear on the need for planning. In fact, Proverbs and Psalms are full of references. Let's look at a few:

Psalm 20:4 (NIV) – "May he give you the desire of your heart and make all your plans succeed."

Proverbs 15:22 (NIV) – "Plans fail for lack of counsel, but with many advisers they succeed."

Proverbs 21:5 (NIV) - The plans of the diligent lead to profit as surely as haste leads to poverty.

As I read the passages above, as well as many other passages, the underlying premise is that there were first plans before there was a potential outcome. Proverbs 15:22 does not read "If you decide to make some plans, then they might fail for lack of counsel."

No! It makes the assumption and the assertion that

there were plans already established. The act of making the plans are essential to each and every one of the above verses and the lessons learned. This process of planning—master planning—must not be passed-over or short-circuited. The plans you develop now will serve you and your team long into the future.

There are a lot of perils in a facility development and master planning process. Your dream can get derailed if your facilities vision is too grandiose. People far from God who could have been reached by your ministry will remain far from God as a result. Families who could have been put back together at your church will remain in conflict because you were not able to develop tools that allowed you to minister effectively to them. Your church could struggle to remain unified and focused because of financial bondage. To be sure, the stakes are high.

As you navigate your way through this book, you will find not only the theory behind master planning, but also some practical tools to help apply the principles to your specific church and ministry. In the appendices you will find some worksheets for you to use with your team as a guide to develop some initial plans.

Prologue:
Pastor Bob's
Frustration

*"Would you tell me which way I ought to go from
here?" asked Alice. "That depends a good deal
on where you want to get," said the Cat.
"I really don't care where," replied Alice.
"Then it doesn't much matter which
way you go," said the Cat.*
— Alice in Wonderland by Lewis Carroll

It had been another frustrating meeting, one in a series of wearisome meetings, and Pastor Bob was exhaust-
ed. Now into his third year as pastor of First Church, Bob
had inherited the leadership of a historic church that was
experiencing a spurt of new life as its downtown location
was beginning to attract young professionals and families.
Bob—a gifted communicator and a people-person—was
well-loved by his congregation. They had been respon-
sive to his efforts to launch new ministries to reach their
rapidly changing community, and the church had experienced significant growth in the last two years.

So much growth had occurred that First Church was fast running out of space. They needed more room for the children's ministry and an expansion of the church offices, and they wanted to update their youth building and worship center. At least, that was what Bob thought.

He assembled a team of congregational leaders to help him turn his dreams into reality and to ensure that First would be able to meet the needs of the many new families with kids and teenagers who were coming to check the church out. The team included contractors, engineers, bankers, and gifted managers. Bob assumed he had a dream team that would help him navigate the planning, design, building, and financial challenges of the upcoming projects. His job, he assumed, was to explain the challenges facing the church, articulate his clear and unique vision for the church's next 20 years, and then let the experts bring it all to pass. Only it had not been quite that easy. Or easy at all, as a matter of fact.

The architects and engineers squabbled. The pastoral staff all insisted that the physical needs of their individual ministry areas had to take center stage. The bankers seemed to delight in throwing a financial wet blanket over every hot, visionary idea Bob came up with. Bob got into the habit of taking a small bottle of Advil to the project team meetings.

After one particularly contentious meeting, Bob trudged back toward his office to gather his briefcase and coat and make the weary drive home. As he left the build-ing, Tom, one of the project team members, asked if he could walk with Pastor Bob to his car. Bob agreed.

"Pastor," Tom began, "I can't help but notice that you seem to be really discouraged by this process. Is there anything I can do to help?" Encouraged by a caring ques-tion from someone not fighting for turf or shooting down ideas, Bob opened up, surprising even himself.

"Tom," he replied, "I am beyond discouraged. I am getting downright depressed. I never knew that this pro-cess was going to be so agonizing. This church has had great unity. The people are wonderful. We are growing. I assumed this building project would be like everything else in the last three years—challenging, but exciting and fun. After all, 'God's work, God's way,' right?"

Bob tossed his briefcase into the backseat and sighed wearily. "Gotta be honest with you, though. I figured that at this point we would have some pretty pictures to show the congregation. You know, cool color drawings, 3D an-imation videos to put on the website and digital signage. I thought my job was just to articulate the vision, to say what needed to be done, and then together we would fig-ure out how to design it, build it, and pay for it. That's a master plan, right? That's what I need: a master plan. Now I am wondering if I need a combination MBA, com-mercial contractor's license, acoustic certification, and architecture degree just to make any sense of this!"

Bob sighed and shook Tom's hand. "Thanks for asking, Tom. Now I've got to get home to the kids." He started to put his key in the ignition, paused, and turned back to his friend. "You know, I just did not know a building project would be this hard and discouraging. I am not even sure I have what it takes to lead First through this." Pastor Bob started his car and drove home.

Chapter One:
Start Right

"Plans are only good intentions unless they immediately degenerate into hard work."
— Peter Drucker

When Pastor Bob said, "I need a master plan," what he really meant was, "I need to have a concrete projection of the future so that I can cast vision and so that we can raise the needed resources to accomplish our ministry." Both goals are worthy ones, and a good master planning process will make them possible. However, like most leaders, Pastor Bob did not fully understand the complexity of the process. In particular, he underestimated the sheer amount of data that must be gathered, evaluated, and processed before a clear picture of the future can emerge.

Simply put, Bob is not exactly sure what master planning actually encompasses. He is not alone. I am writing this book to help leaders just like Bob have clarity and confidence when it comes to navigating the master-planning process. Let's start with a working definition.

My definition incorporates three dimensions:

- A programmatic study of current and long-range ministry initiatives, and if/how facilities may or may not assist in accomplishing those plans.
- A vision of the future, beginning with today's realities.
- A clear and intentional big-picture view of the ministry's future based upon a ministry's needs, hopes, culture, DNA, and desires.

Let's look at each of these dimensions in detail.

A PROGRAMMATIC STUDY

A master plan, by definition, requires thoroughness. In order to analyze a ministry's paradigm, the stakeholders must collect data, carry out research, perform due diligence, and ask lots of pointed questions. It is impossible to plan wisely without a comprehensive review of a ministry's current context, resources, story, vision, and capabilities.

Practically, what might this look like? Let's say that our family agrees it is time for us to take a vacation. We are all in agreement that we need a break, but that is where the consensus ends. We're not sure where to go, what we should do when we get there, when we should depart and return, and how much money we should spend. We need to do extensive research, seek the input of the involved parties, and consider their desires and needs. We also need to review our available resources in order to set a budget and take our kids desires and needs into consideration.

My wife and I consult our "cherubs" (though our children are not always "angels" by any stretch!), dive into the process, and come up with these initial findings:

- We want to go to the mountains. We love the mountains and even hope to live there one day. We could go to the beach, to a large city, or to an amusement park but, for this vacation, the mountains are the right choice.

- We want to stay for a week. Any less time and we will not be fully rested and rejuvenated. Any longer and we would start to get on each other's nerves.

- We have arrived at a feasible dollar amount for our trip budget. We know how much cash we have on hand and how much we are willing to finance with credit cards.

So, are we are ready to leave? Not quite. We still have some important questions to answer. Which mountains? Do we want to stay in a log cabin, a house, a condo, a hotel, a camper, or a tent?

Which week is the best, based on any potential conflicts with our family's schedule related to school, sports, church activities, and music lessons? How much vacation time do we have available from work? How much of our available resources should we allocate for lodging? Gas?

Food? Entertainment? How much should we keep in reserve in case of an emergency? What is the right mode of transportation to get us there?

Once we've answered all these questions, it must be time to start packing, right? Not even close! We still have more research to do. This next phase of planning the trip is the most challenging. This is where wishes and desires come face to face with reality. It is the moment of compromise.

We would love to stay at a five-star resort with a full day-spa and all the amenities, but our budget will allow only an RV or condo. My wife and I would love to dine out for every meal in fine dining establishments, but our budget says only one restaurant meal per day. The kids would be thrilled to experience the amusement parks or activities that require an extra fee, but in reality, hiking at the national park and swimming in the lake are all that we can afford.

> **If we could first know where we are, and whither we are tending, we could better judge what to do, and how to do it.**
>
> — Abraham Lincoln

You have probably planned family vacations in a similar manner. Such preparation is second nature for most of us. For some reason, however, ministries tend to skip over this sort of due diligence and intentional research. Without the strong foundation laid by this critical phase, ministries can flounder and encounter severe financial challenges.

A FUTURE VISION BASED ON TODAY'S REALITIES

The second dimension of master planning involves a vision of the future firmly rooted in the realities of today. We must face our current realities while balancing them with assumptions about the future. Let's stick with our vacation analogy for a moment. The vision of our mountain getaway that is beginning to emerge is based solidly on an honest assessment of our current realities. For example:

- We assume everyone is going to be healthy. They are right now . . . but what if? If someone gets sick, the whole vacation may have to be canceled or postponed.
- We assume that the price of gasoline will remain fairly consistent. If there is a 20-30% spike in gas costs, the entire trip could come into question.
- We assume the family car is roadworthy (we even

plan to have it serviced before we leave). If we have a flat tire or an accident, it could throw off our budget and the timing of the vacation.

- We assume our lodging reservations will be honored. If there is a mix-up, or a fire, or the hotel goes out of business, could we easily find other available accommodations at an affordable price? Or would we have to rethink all of our plans?

This list is obviously not inclusive of all potential scenarios. There are many other issues that could arise. Master planning is, of course, about the future. And the future is unpredictable. Experienced planners don't have crystal balls enabling them to predict the future with absolute certainty. Instead, we include contingency plans, taking into account the "what if" questions. This does not mean we are pessimistic or frightened. It simply means we are honest and prudent.

A Big Picture View of the Future

We are nearly ready to pack the car and head to the mountains, where the air is crisp and the temperature is 20 degrees cooler! Before the garage door goes up, however, we have one more dimension of our plan to consider: the specific details that will finish the picture of our vacation painted in broad strokes.

Where will we eat when we splurge on a restaurant, and what sorts of meals will we cook? Where will we stop along the way? What sites do we want to see? What do we hope our vacation does for our family relationally, spiritually, and emotionally?

A good master plan, like a good vacation, requires a lot of preparation, thought, research, "what if" planning, and discussion. A bad vacation features empty wallets, late arrivals, unplanned-for crises, and a grumpy family. A bad master plan can result in frustrated expectations, financial shortfalls, divided leadership, and decades of regret.

In fact, I would contend that the proverbial "master plan" actually is comprised of four master plans. Each one building a foundation that leads to the next with confidence and clarity. Just as we saw in our vacation analogy, each phase of the trip required a disciplined and focused exercise of asking questions, research, study, expertise, and vision clarity.

In his insightful book, *Church Unique*, Will Mancini describes clarity this way:

"What is Clarity really about? A synthesis of definitions brings clarity to the concept of clarity: it means being free from anything that obscures, blocks, pollutes, or darkens. Being clear as a leader means being simple, understandable, and exact. The leader helps others see and understand reality better. Leaders constantly bring the most important things to light: Current reality and future possibilities, what

God says about it and what we need to do about it."

Do you have this level of clarity at your church?

Is your church staff, leadership, and congregation clear on the "why" of what you do? Without the clarity of direction, people start to question, "What is this all about?" or "Why are we doing this?" or worse, "I sure hope the pastor/elders know what they are doing."

In general, organizations suffer from a lack of vision clarity either because the leader fails to communicate it effectively or people simply don't trust the leader enough. Your church needs to believe that the leaders understand the vision and have prayed about it. Your church should know that you've thought through the "why" and established strategies for the "how." They need to believe . . . they *want* to believe in the direction and leadership of the church. They want their leaders to communicate confidently that this is where we are going and here is why. As a leader, if you do not hear your people reiterate the vision or make comments like "we can do this," then it may be a sign the vision has not be adequately conveyed, communicated, or embraced.

Far too many churches think that they have clarity because they have a mission statement. They plaster it on the lobby wall, put it on the website, and cover the back of their business cards, all while not knowing exactly who they are and why they exist. Yet if you ask them if the community would miss them if they ceased to exist, they cannot respond affirmatively.

Vision statements can be incredibly powerful tools to rally your congregation around the vision and calling . . . if it truly represents the vision. Or, they can be incredibly obtuse statements that make people dose off, yawn, and become numb. The primary difference is if your vision/ mission statement is crystal clear and is a call to action versus just making a statement of belief or theology. The rest of this book will show you how to prevent such a disaster from distracting your ministry. We'll specifically drill down into each of the four master plans:

1. Ministry Master Plan
2. Financial Master Plan
3. Facility Master Plan
4. Sustaining Master Plan

Let's head for the mountains!

CHAPTER TWO:
FROM THE INSIDE
OUT—THE MINISTRY
MASTER PLAN

"Suppose one of you wants to build a tower. Will he not first sit down and estimate the cost to see if he has enough money to complete it? For if he lays the foundation and is not able to finish it, everyone who sees it will ridicule him, saying, 'This fellow began to build and was not able to finish.'"
— Jesus Christ (Luke 14:28–30)

In my many years working with churches, I have watched more than once as a promising master planning process becomes a train wreck. At the beginning, there is a sense of excitement. Possibilities for the future seem limitless. The ministry leaders genuinely want to serve God, and people are full of enthusiasm. Then something goes wrong. Friends are at odds. A project is dramatically over budget. Ministry dreams slowly die.

More often than not, this slow death happens when a ministry shortchanges the first, and most crucial, part of the master planning process: the exploration and discovery of philosophies, concepts, stories, and cultural context through intentional research. We have to start from the inside out. For the sake of simplicity, I'll call this critical first stage the "Ministry Master Plan." It is the plan that helps identify the *who* (we are), the *why* (we do what we do) and the *how* (we do ministry). It is the first of four master plans (or master plan processes) that must be incorporated if your church is going to have a meaningful and successful outcome.

To skip over this process of ministry master planning is like getting the GO TO JAIL card in Monopoly. You do not pass go; you do not collect $200. Actually, skipping this part of the process is more damaging and expensive. This step is the foundation of the rest of the processes. Avoiding the Ministry Master Plan will leave the other three plans on unstable ground.

Over the years, I have come to realize that there are seven critical questions every church must ask before launching a building project. Key team members in each ministry area must answer and analyze these questions during the ministry master planning process:

- What is your vision for ministry?
- Who is our "target" in this ministry?
- What is our DNA as a ministry?
- How do we define "value" for our ministry?
- What is our "story," and how should it be communicated?

- If space and finances were not an issue, what ministries would we start or expand?
- If we do *not* start or expand the above ministries, what kind of impact will that decision have on our community?

Let's explore each of these seven critical questions.

WHAT IS YOUR VISION FOR MINISTRY?

The two key words in this question are "your" and "vision." They are specific and personal to your ministry. The vision is where you, as the leader of the ministry, believe God wants you to take his work.

A thousand policemen directing traffic cannot tell you why you come or where you go.
— T.S. Elliott

Remember, this is *your* vision. No one else can tell you what your vision should be. No architect, builder, consultant, or friend can tell you what your vision is. This vision is unique to you because God has given it to you. Obviously, God may use others in this process, but as the ministry leader, you are the gatekeeper of the vision. The team you assemble to assist you through this process can help you decipher how that vision affects other areas of the church (finances, facilities, land development, among others), but they cannot determine God's vision for your ministry. Of course, wise leaders will seek input from trusted counselors, but it is up to the leaders to identify, defend, and articulate God's vision.

Where do you see God leading you this year? Next year? Five or ten years from now? If you can clearly articulate the vision and make it personal, then you are ready to continue. If you can't, you should turn to God and seek his vision. Dream big. But yield to God's plans. He will always take you and your ministry to the exact right place. You might find that professional strategic consulting and planning will help at this juncture.

WHO IS OUR "TARGET" IN THIS MINISTRY?

For some, talk of churches having a "target market" is ridiculous. Some might even go so far as to say a "target" is not biblical. After all, isn't the good news message for all people? Isn't targeting a certain type of person a secular pursuit unworthy of the gospel of Christ? Isn't our job to take the good word to all people, not just a niche audience?

Please don't misunderstand me. I am not suggesting

that we forgo the Great Commission or that we ignore certain groups of people. Keep in mind the idea of a target market is not outside biblical parameters. Consider Paul. Paul's mission was to share the word of saving grace provided to us through a personal relationship with Jesus Christ. As we study Paul's letters, we see that he understood each audience he addressed, and was able to tailor his message to their needs without ever changing the truth of the gospel. While his message didn't vary, Paul addressed the Greeks differently than he did Jews. Why? Because the Greeks and Jews were different "target markets." Each had different backgrounds and foundations, and they needed to be addressed in a manner that considered their context. Paul was the master of contextualization. So I use the term "target" not as a marketing ploy to sell something but rather as a way to contextualize the gospel.

Today, every church has a target market, whether or not the church thinks in those terms. My parents come from a traditional background and appreciate a worship setting with pews, hymnals, a pastor in a suit and tie, and a Sunday school program. They seek a fellowship of believers who subscribe to those same desires and values. I am thankful that they have found a church whose ministries "target" these desires. Many people, of all ages and backgrounds, share their preferences.

On the other hand, my family attends a church with a

target different from my parent's church. Our pastor wears jeans and t-shirts, and we dress in shorts and flip-flops. We enjoy chest-pounding, heart-pumping "rock-and-roll" worship with a congregation whose average age is much younger than that of many other churches in the area.

So recognize your target. What kind of person do you reach most effectively? What are the demographics of your community? Who is already sitting in your congregation, and what does that mean to your programs and methodologies and staffing? Are your ministries and philosophy of worship the best to reach this target? Before moving on, it is important that you wrestle with these questions, perhaps with your leadership team. At times the discussion may be tough, but the emerging clarity will be worth it!

WHAT IS OUR DNA AS A MINISTRY?

If you watch any popular television show dealing with forensic science and police work, you are certain to hear the term "DNA." The American Heritage New Dictionary of Cultural Literacy defines DNA as "the molecule that carries information in all living systems."

DNA is the molecular component that identifies each living being specifically, coding the biological components that make each of us unique. No two people have the exact same DNA. This also applies to ministry organizations as well. There are no two ministries exactly alike. There is a uniqueness that is similar to our fingerprints. There may be similarities, but there are still differences, even if they are only subtle. Some uniqueness is by happenstance, location, congregational makeup, or even leadership passion, while others might be referred to as an "intentional difference".

I recently had the privilege to serve on a jury. The case was sensitive and grueling. For six days I listened, along with 13 other jurors, to testimony and viewed evidence. It was demanding yet enlightening. I assure you that the trial process and the crime scene investigators are not like those depicted on television and movies. However, there was DNA evidence that was presented, testified about, and challenged. The primary witness was an analyst from the crime lab that was a DNA expert.

As part of her testimony, she provided us with an incredible amount of scientific details, facts, and figures. She walked us through the process of collecting and testing samplings from the parties involved. She then explained the process of determining probability of DNA matches from one sampling to another . . . from one person to another.

Then came the clincher. It was not only factual and convincing, but also a little humorous. The prosecution asked the DNA expert what the statistical probability for the DNA match to be someone else other than the defendant. There was a match of DNA from samplings from the victim and the defendant. According to the DNA expert, it was an exact match. She then testified that in order to find another person that would have a statistical match to the defendant the likelihood would be 1:35,000,000,000,000. They would have to test 35 trillion people to get the same DNA. I was shocked to hear trillion with a "t." The prosecutor continued by asking the expert how many people are on earth. The answer? Six billion. Despite the gravity of the case, I found her answer humorous. Slam Dunk! Here's my point—your church is unique. About 400,000 churches exist in the United States. Each one is different than the other.

So what is your ministry's DNA? What makes you unique from every other ministry in the world, or other ministries in your church? What are your "molecular markers?" There are foundational elements built within your ministry that make it unique. If your ministry was a cell and we put it under a microscope side by side with other cells, then what would set you apart and make you unique? You must decode your DNA and find out if that DNA aligns with your vision and target. If you are acting in a way not consistent with your DNA, your vision for the future will prove difficult, if not impossible, to reach.

HOW DO WE DEFINE "VALUE" FOR OUR MINISTRY?

"Value" is an increasingly popular term in the business world, although it does not mean the same thing to all who use it. Some people think of value as synonymous with cost. Others equate value with significance, such as a valuable relationship. Many use the term "value-added," which refers to an extra quality of a service or product that you may not be paying for directly.

What does your ministry value? This will be a specific thing or group of things that you, as a leader, believe brings great worth or meaning to your ministry. Some of the things you value may be altruistic, humanitarian, deeply spiritual, emotional, and even physical . . . as in our surroundings and facilities. Does your ministry value stained-glass windows and soaring beamed ceilings, or does it value the ability to get the most possible square footage at the least possible cost, regardless of the aesthetics? Perhaps your ministry values a large choir and great acoustics, or a cozy schoolroom where the youngest members gather for children's Bible study. Whatever you choose as your value priority, recognize that this commitment will shape the course of your master plan in profound ways.

The value question is related to your story. What do you want your ministry to "say" to the community God has placed you in? Spreading your message is not merely a verbal act. The way you allocate your resources, the appearance and design of your physical plant, your choices about community involvement—these are all ways of sharing what is most important to you.

It is particularly important that your budget be aligned with your values. Take a look at your church budget and your spending to date in order to examine if the way you spend the resources God has entrusted you matches your vision and story. Are you investing these funds in the areas that will help you minister to the target market God has given you the passion to reach? We'll cover more on finances later. But for now consider the above question.

> **The significant problems we face cannot be solved at the same level of thinking we were at when we created them.**
> — Albert Einstein

WHAT IS YOUR "STORY," AND HOW SHOULD IT BE COMMUNICATED?

Story is all around us. It is everywhere we look. We cannot escape the impact that story has on our everyday lives and interactions. We as humans tell a story. Every new moment becomes a different page. We can walk into a room and people start to "read" our story. How we interact communicates much of what we value and how we see the world around us. The same applies to our facilities. They tell a story. Does your facility tell a story that supports . . .

1. Our vision and mission?
2. Who we are trying to reach?
3. Our community?
4. Who we are?
5. What we value?

If your story is not in lockstep with these elements—stop! A prerequisite to effective ministry is congruence at every level. You must bring the vision, target, DNA, values, and story into alignment with every choice you make. While the first five questions require us to dig deep into who we believe God has called us to be, the next two questions start to address the desires of our hearts and the passions that motivates us.

IF SPACE AND FINANCES WERE NOT AN ISSUE, WHAT MINISTRIES WOULD WE START OR EXPAND?

If you had all of the physical space you could ever want and an unlimited budget, what ministries would you enlarge? What new endeavors would you likely start? What would it take to make them a reality? How much space would it take? How many volunteers would you need? How long would it take to implement?

This is the part of the process where you get to dream. Remember, a master plan is a "big picture" process. Ask all of your senior leadership and individual ministry leaders this question. You may be surprised at the passion and creativity that can flow from people's hearts once they are given the opportunity to express themselves. However, remember that this part of the process must still come into alignment with your responses to the first five questions. Your dreaming must harmonize with your vision, target, DNA, values, and story.

> **The plans of the diligent lead surely to advantage, but everyone who is hasty comes surely to poverty.**
> — Proverbs 21:5

IF WE DO NOT START OR EXPAND THE ABOVE MINISTRIES, WHAT KIND OF IMPACT WILL THAT DECISION HAVE ON OUR COMMUNITY?

This question is the most subjective of the seven, which may make it the most challenging. To answer it, you will have to indulge in a bit of speculation about what might happen if your ministry fails to enhance or develop the ministries you envision as your goal. If we believe that our vision, target, and DNA are all aligned with our understanding of what God is leading us to do, and we are not able to accomplish these things, then what is the impact? What are the opportunities lost?

These are eternal questions, not merely part of a business plan. We are talking about people's lives and spiritual development. It is important that we find the best and most thorough way to influence the lives of those whom God has called us to reach. This is a serious matter—one that, I know, you do not take lightly.

The master planning process begins when we answer these questions with honesty and courage. I mean courage in the literal sense. It is frightening to dig beneath the surface and unearth issues that are uncomfortable and possibly threatening. It is always easier to maintain the status quo than to wrestle with understanding our values and beliefs. Being a ministry leader is a hard enough calling. Why invite the pain of a possible disagreement over philosophy and values?

However, I want to challenge you to consider what would have happened if Jesus had chosen to go with the flow rather than to confront the most important issues at hand. What if Saul had not followed Christ, changed his name to Paul, and ruffled more than a few feathers? What if Moses had come down from the mountain and said, "I know I have met with God and he has given me these great commandments but, hey, the people are so happy worshipping these idols . . . why should I rock the boat?"

As the church of Jesus Christ, we do not have the luxury of going with the flow or maintaining the status quo. We have been called by Jesus to be "salt and light." No Christian has a passive calling. We are to be active in the world. It requires courageous action, and action, in turn, requires planning.

Your answers to the seven questions will be different in many ways from any other ministry's answers, because God has created you, a unique being in a unique church. Whatever your answers, wrestle with the questions wisely and intentionally, as they are the very foundation of master planning. Now it's time to move from the realm of values and philosophy to the realm of finances—another important part of master planning! But first, let's check in with our friend Pastor Bob.

CHAPTER THREE: COUNTING THE COST—THE FINANCIAL MASTER PLAN

"By failing to prepare, you prepare to fail."
— Benjamin Franklin

You know, honey," Bob told his wife Karen at dinner one night, "I can't believe how far we have come in just six months. Last winter I was nearly ready to pack it up and go find something to sell for a living. I was really at the end of my rope. But this new project team has breathed some life back into me. I don't think we are out of the woods yet, or that we have everything figured out, but I can actually feel some hope for the first time in a while."

Karen smiled at her husband. "You know, I can really see the difference in you. Tom's friend has really helped, hasn't he?"

The morning after Bob had left the dark church parking lot in despair, Tom had called him. He gave his pastor the phone number of a friend who worked to help churches navigate the master-planning process. Reluctant at first, Bob agreed to meet with the consultant, and eventually introduced him to other senior members of the project team. Together they agreed to invite the consultant to help facilitate (Bob had never like that word, but now he was coming to understand it) their master-planning process.

To be honest, the process had moved more slowly than Bob had wanted. There were nights when he wanted to pound the conference room table and cry, "Let's get on with this!" The consultant was covering topics such as vision, strategy, and DNA—topics about which Bob assumed the entire leadership team had consensus. After all, the church had clear documents about such things.

However, over time, Bob discovered that just because a document has been written and approved does not mean all involved agree with it and understand it. One eye-opening discussion had come when the consultant challenged the team to talk about their "target market."

Bob was ready with an answer. "Well, we are really clear about that. We are targeting young families between the ages of thirty and forty who live within a three-mile radius of our church." Much to Bob's surprise, an older member of the team then cleared his throat and began to speak, at first hesitantly but with growing warmth.

"Pastor, I know young families are important. After all, children represent the future of our church. Still, sometimes I think we appear a bit exclusive. Jesus died for *all* people. And didn't Paul say that he had become all things to all people so that some might be saved? I have some qualms about focusing on just one market, when many diverse communities out there need to know Christ!"

Bob was taken aback, but it was soon clear that others felt the same way. At first, the pastor wanted to drown out the questioning voices with logic and reason. When that proved futile, he wanted to ask if they had been paying attention when he was in the role of vision-caster. One dark night he confided in Karen that he was considering resigning because he wasn't sure that the other leaders of the church believed in his vision for ministry.

Over a period of weeks, though, the heat of the initial discussions transformed into the light of increased clarity and unity. The project team came to a new understanding of their vision, DNA, and story as a church. After long discussions—often difficult ones—about what the church valued and what was non-essential, the leaders forged a real and growing consensus about the meanings of words they had used for years.

The real turning point had come the night the consultant looked around the room and addressed the leaders, speaking slowly and firmly. "I need to ask you to wrestle with a hard question. You are coming to some clarity about your target, DNA, values, story, and vision. You have done great work! But now you have to answer a scary question. What if you don't live those things out? What if you don't make the strategic adaptations that will enable you to fulfill your calling? What is the cost to your church? To this community? What if you miss what God has for you?"

There was a long silence. When it passed, however, the group began a long and fruitful discussion. For the first time, the leaders were not attempting to define and clarify ideals, or to defend positions. Rather, they began to take into account the cost of ministry success or failure. Suddenly, they was not a collection of representatives advocating for different philosophies and ministry areas. They were one team, rallying for a common purpose, working toward a common destiny.

Dinner ended and Bob began to clear the dishes. "You know, Karen," he mused, "there is a lot I don't understand yet about this process. There are some baffling technical issues about vision, mission, story, and physical requirements I—that is, *we* have to grapple with. We have a long way to go. But just coming this far, I can see how we, as a church, can get to where we are going together."

He paused as he filled the dishwasher: "I like the sound of *together*." The team was coming together. But another part of the process loomed just ahead of them—the financial master plan.

The financial master plan is the second most important master plan that your church will need to develop. Once you have developed your ministry master plan, you need to determine the financial feasibility of the short-term vision and long-term vision. What is needed to fulfill the ministry master plan from a payroll perspective? How will it impact the budget? Is the ministry master plan financially sustainable? Are facilities required to meet the plan? If so, given our financial status, what can the church afford?

The following steps will help you develop a financial master plan. As a word of caution, do not skip over this step in the process. The tendency is to go right to the facility master plan, but this second step is critically important. Without the perspective of the financial master plan, your facility master plan could be dead in the water. While dreaming big and having a God-sized plan are important, financial prudence is also a biblical part of this process. If you give stewardship lip service, then you will have plans and pretty pictures that never become reality.

FINANCIAL EVALUATION

Financial evaluation is a critical, albeit often-overlooked, part of the master planning process. Because ministry leaders hold such a strong belief in the power of their vision, these leaders often assume that once the vision is communicated, the financial resources will automatically follow. But this is no wiser than leaving for

a family vacation without enough cash on hand to provide lodging, gas, and food. Since most churches plan
on incorporating the earliest phases of their master plan
in the near future, financial analysis must be taken into
consideration and is, in fact, one of the key drivers of the
process.

In more than 28 years of helping ministries to develop
their facilities, I have yet to work with any church or ministry organization that did not need money to build. They
either needed cash to build their ministry tools or needed
to borrow some or all of the funds. I have yet to find a
builder who was willing to exchange manna for building
materials. As a result, I have found it extraordinarily helpful to talk about the distinction between fact and faith.

FACT OR FAITH?

"The bank has told us that we can borrow whatever
we need." I have heard those words uttered by many a
well-meaning church leader. However, they may not mean
exactly what they seem. The reality is that the bank means
that you can borrow whatever you need as long as it is
within your payback capability, which takes into account
the value of your property and its future improvements
as well as your assets and cash flow. Hence, you need to
make sure you have adequately determined your budget

for the project. In almost every case, churches are faced with a decision between fact and faith. Let's work through some practical examples.

When I talk about facts, here are some of the examples of components that would influence the fact side of the ledger:

- We have 500 people
- We have $100,000 in a contingency fund
- Our annual income is $900,000
- Our giving has increased 5% a year for the past three years
- Our land has a value of $1 million
- Our current 30,000 square footage is worth $4 million
- We have no debt

The facts, in this case, are simply what we know. The facts include numerical criteria and forecast what we can afford today. We count the liquid funds on hand and the income from tithes and offerings. We can run some projections based on the number of people in attendance and the average increase (or decrease) in our giving over the past three years. We also have other assets—our current land, physical plant, and stocks. Then we have our liabilities—how much debt are we encumbered by, or other long-term obligations that are a drain on cash-flow. Those are some of the constants, the facts that a bank would look at in determining whether they would lend money to your church for a capital improvement initiative.

The faith side is a bit more ambiguous. It takes into account unknowns that we trust the Lord will provide for us, such as the potential commitments in a capital stewardship campaign, the desire to sell a piece of property that the church owns, the possibility of a large single-donor contribution, or some other source outside of regular tithes and offerings. What is taken on faith has a tendency to vary with each ministry, and can have a great influence on how a project is designed. If a church believes that they can run a capital campaign and generate four times the church's annual income, and they are willing to borrow 100% against those funds, that would indicate a high faith threshold (probably too aggressive). On the other hand, if a church does not plan on doing a capital campaign despite having no other means by which to gather resources, then that would be a low faith threshold. Every church needs to examine itself to determine its comfort level between faith and fact, and the project needs to be envisioned with that balance in mind.

I strongly recommend that every church work on their master plans with some level of faith in mind. God honors our expressions of faith in him. At the same time, if the church has an extremely high level of faith, the congregation should also make the prudent choice of creating a backup plan. A great method for this is dividing a project into multiple phases so that if, for some reason, the funds do not materialize as expected, the project need not be shelved. Too many churches who have planned based on a high faith line have spent tens of thousands of dollars on drawings that were based on dreams, "blue sky" thinking, and aggressive faith assumptions. They have come up short. This type of poor planning can demoralize a congregation and weaken its leadership.

There has been an old rule of thumb that a church can borrow about three times its annual income. While that is a fair starting point for preliminary budgeting, it is not enough to determine definitively what the church can afford. Three times the annual income of a church that is already spending its entire budget is a meaningless number, because there is no margin for additional payments or expenditures. In the same way, a church with a large debt load cannot count on the "three times" rule.

A slightly more realistic, but similar, rule is that a church can afford to complete a project that is based on three times its annual income, less debt, plus cash. This rule is still not perfectly reliable, as current budget spending versus current giving and income calculations may skew the equation.

So, what is a good rule of thumb that represents a responsible balance between fact and faith? I believe that every church should consider a capital stewardship campaign, or better-stated, a generosity initiative. Such initiatives not only raise money for a specific project, but also tend to grow the faith and generosity of members. They also provide leadership a perfect opportunity to communicate the principles of biblical stewardship. A capital stewardship campaign that could raise 1.5-2 times a church's annual income is a responsible, conservative, and attainable goal. This is far less than most stewardship campaign companies would indicate but is a range that I have found to be conservative. This number assumes you engage a professional stewardship consulting firm, as the average for an "in-house" campaign is closer to less than 1.0 times a church's annual income.

If you assume that 1.7 times your income is a reasonable goal, I encourage you to assume that you will actually collect 75-80% of the amount pledged. There are a number of reasons:

- Some people relocate, so they no longer give to the church they once attended
- Some people will lose jobs, are displaced, or otherwise have to change occupations, which causes financial challenges
- Lifestyle changes have an impact on giving (kids go to college; someone is in an accident; an elderly parent requires care)
- Others will become disillusioned for whatever reason and either stop giving or actually leave the church

Given these factors, let's use an 80% collectible estimate for discussion purposes. Let's also assume that this 80% will be collected over a three-year period. Now take the 80% and divide it by thirty-six months to establish the amount of "income" that a bank might use when considering a church's financial assets (over and above the operating budget). This "cushion" is necessary collateral; it can be used for any possible debt services during the project. But you need to talk to your lender before too many assumptions are made.

It is important here to note the difference between debt service and debt retirement. In most cases, churches utilize a capital campaign to do one of two things: generate an infusion of cash as a sort of "first fruits" of a longer campaign, or to build cash-flow for debt servicing.

A ministry's first campaign associated with a specific project is generally used for debt servicing, while subsequent campaigns are then required for debt retirement. Make sure that your congregation is clear on this point. If your desire is to use the capital campaign funds either to retire your debt or to pay in cash for the project, then you will need to postpone the project until all of the monies have been collected. While I have seen this work in a few instances, there are significant challenges. First, you would need to consider the cost of inflation. If you intend to build a $3 million project, and you have commitments for all $3 million (based on 80% collected), but you intend to wait for the entire amount to be collected over three years of your campaign, then you are going to wind up short in three years. If construction inflation were to increase at a rate of 3% per year, you could be looking at an additional $270,000 that you would need to raise just to keep up with inflation. If that requires you to delay the project another year to raise the added funds, then you will need to raise another $90,000 for the added year. Don't be surprised if you feel like a hamster on a wheel, never reaching the goal, and thus, never starting the project.

Another issue is the loss of momentum. It has been my experience that people give to see something happen, and when it is delayed, they lose motivation to continue giving. The momentum of, and enthusiasm for, the project dries up (or slows to a trickle) until they see some dirt moving or other activity on the site.

Finally, consider the opportunity loss of the ministry: If your ministry has reached a point of facility saturation—which may be why you are considering an expansion in the first place—consider the opportunities lost by not providing the facilities to accomplish ministry. If you wait three years to have all the cash on hand before you start to build, you could be four or more years away from being able to utilize the facility. At that point, will you still need the facility? Will the people you had hoped to serve have found another place to meet their needs?

Let's take our ratio and run the numbers for a case study. First, we will assume that a church has an annual budget of $900,000. Given our ratio, we could estimate total commitments of $1,530,000 ($900,000 x 1.7). Eighty percent of that total number is $1,224,000 so we can assume that that is the amount we have to use during the capital campaign, at the rate of collection of $34,000 per month. That amount of money, at an interest rate of 6% amortized over twenty-five years, would allow the church to service a loan in the amount of approximately $5.3 million.

DISCLAIMER

I am not a generosity nor a stewardship specialist. Also, many of the church lending institutions have adjusted their lending practices since the most recent recession. "Theoretical" campaign commitments may not be considered for future debt service, so cash and debt service margins within your normal operational budget can be the more prudent way to calculate lending limits. In addition, most lenders now are looking for a campaign track record before they would consider the campaign dollars as an offset for cash-flow, usually 6-12 months of receivables. I strongly recommend that you seek the counsel of a lender and stewardship specialist.

Now you see how the numbers work and what sort of contribution levels you can expect using the fact and faith continuum. What's next if you are considering a facility development initiative? What needs to be considered if your evaluations tell you that the solution is some type of facility? The next step is to determine your *total project budget*. This is a term that is confused with a similar term, *building budget*. What is the difference?

The building budget is just that—the budget to build the structures from the footings up. On the other hand, the total project budget includes the projected cost for *every aspect* of the project, including the building of the structures. What are these aspects, in addition to actual construction costs? The following is a representative list of such items:

TOTAL PROJECT BUDGET ITEMS

- Civil engineering and other survey and geotechnical services
- Architecture and engineering fees
- Project facilitator/Owner's rep
- Permit costs
- Property insurance (commonly referred to as builder's risk insurance)
- Legal assistance
- Specialty engineering services (landscape architect, commercial kitchen, etc.)
- Acoustical, video, lighting, and acoustic (AVLA) design

- Interior design
- Thematic design and implementation
- Furniture, fixtures, and equipment
- Cost of AVLA systems
- Technology/IT design and implementation
- Capital stewardship campaign costs, including multi-media
- Demolition/renovation cost
- Inflationary contingency
- Design and construction contingency
- Financing cost (loan fees, title insurance, points, etc.)
- Permit expediting services
- Site work, grading, utilities, paving, etc.
- Landscaping

I advise ministry leaders that they can expect that these items will consume 45-60% of the total project budget. This means that a church would only have 40-55%, give or take for the actual construction costs, for the construction of the "building." So when I hear a ministry leader say, "We want to build a $3 million project," I always ask if they mean a $3 million building or total project. If it is the latter, that would lead me to believe that they will have $1.2–1.7 million to spend on the actual building. Too many ministries don't understand this difference and suffer a nasty sticker shock a few steps into the process. I don't want that to happen to you!

Chapter Four:
From the Outside
In—The Facility
Master Plan, Part A

"I've often thought that if our zoning boards could
be put in charge of botanists, of zoologists and geolo-
gists, and people who know about the earth, we would
have much more wisdom in such planning than
we have when we leave it up to the engineers."
— William O. Douglas, Supreme Court Justice (1898–1980)

"LORD HAVE MERCY," Pastor Bob thought to himself as he starred glassy eyed at the list of regulations the county official had given him. "We just want to add some new ministry facilities to our campus, I had no idea that there were these many hoops," he said to the semi-interested government employee who stood stoically behind the counter with little more than a nod of the head to confirm the complexity of the process.

As Pastor Bob walked out of the foreboding building department office, he thought to himself, "I did not go

to seminary to deal with things like environmental studies, wetlands, setbacks, and all the rest of this. I want to
preach the gospel and help people. Who dreams up all
of this stuff?" He then reached for his phone to call Tom
to talk with him on what appeared to be a daunting set
of tasks.

"Hey Tom, this is Pastor Bob. Do you have a minute to
chat? I really needs some help."

"Sure thing," Tom said. "Is everything OK? Are you
hurt or sick? Is your family OK?"

Yeah, yeah, everyone is fine . . . well except for me, at
the moment." Pastor Bob continued, "I just left the building department and I feel completely overwhelmed. Did
you know that we cannot even cut down a tree on the
property that we own without a permit and county approval? Are you aware that the county has one regulation
and ordinance after another that is going to take more
time and money to get accomplished? What is going on?"

There was a slight pause while Pastor Bob caught his
breathe, then Tom jumped back in. "Pastor, calm down.
Count to 10 and then we can talk."

"Seven, eight, nine, ten," Tom could hear lightly over
the phone.

"OK . . . I am calm. Can we get together for coffee? I
can get to your favorite shop on 30 minutes."

"Absolutely. See you then," Tom replied assuredly.

"Let me have a large latte with and an extra shot. Make

that two extra shots, this could be a long day," Pastor Bob said to the server behind the counter. With his beverage of choice in hand, he made his way to the back corner table where Tom was already sipping on his own cup of java.

"Tom, I must admit that my head is spinning." Pastor Bob continued, "The DNA stuff and vision clarity work we did was fun. I got a kick out of seeing the team gel and watch the lightbulbs of focus and direction get switched on. But this stuff . . ." Pastor Bob paused and starred at Tom who sat calm and did not react to Bob's comments. "How does anyone ever get a project built with all of this red tape and regulations?" Bob asked. "How do we move from the vision to this next phase?"

Tom sat calmly and then leaned toward Pastor Bob, "It is definitely a complex set of requirements," Tom said as he proofed the list of county regulations Pastor Bob had laid on the table. "But you know what, I'm not freaked out about this. Do you remember the consultant we engaged to help us with the DNA and visioning process? He warned us this was coming. He told us there was a lot more to this process than we thought." The two men's eyes locked and Pastor Bob's countenance became solemn. Bob can remember the conversation with the consultant after the visioning process: "We got it from here . . . we know a guy."

There was silence for a few seconds. Then Bob said in a humble voice, "You are right. He warned us, but we thought we could handle this. We thought 'How hard can this be?'"

Tom nodded his head affirming Pastor Bob's comments. "Now I get it. There is a lot to this, and we are not prepared. Remember the consultant using the analogy of a whitewater rafting trip. He said that we could buy a guide book and try to figure it out on our own, or we could have a seasoned guide lead us down the river. We do not have the time, expertise, or resources to get this done or lead the process." At this point, Tom was grinning from ear to ear with a fatherly look in his eyes as if his son had finally grasped a necessary life lesson.

"Pastor," Tom said, "Do you think we should call the consultant back and have a discussion about these next steps? I am sure he would welcome our call."

"No doubt! Do you have his number?"

₧₨

Let me give you a heads up. This chapter is more technical in nature. Some ministry professionals might struggle with the amount of technical detail in this chapter. You have probably received training in teaching, leading, and caring for the souls of the people God has entrusted you to lead. Many of you may not necessarily have formal training in the business-oriented aspects of leading a ministry. You know that your ministry's physical plant is important, but more than likely, you have neither the inclination nor the desire to master details about municipal codes, easements, equitable liens, and water retention issues. I could be wrong, but I'm guessing most of you do not consider these things a hobby.

But I assure you this information is important. Please don't skip over this material because you have a compelling vision and you assume everything else will fall in line as a result. That mindset, though understandable, is a sign of a fatal mistake: living by faith while ignoring facts (more on the faith/fact dichotomy later). In the master-planning process, both faith and facts are of crucial importance.

I have compiled a list of many of the items that you must address before any concept drawings can be developed. In most cases, your project team should be commissioned to gather this data on behalf of the church, leadership, and the ministry. Do not feel as if you or your leadership has to obtain this on your own.

If you are a ministry professional, your most significant contribution during this phase of the process is likely to be the selection of the right members for your team: men and women who bring expertise and experience in areas where you have not necessarily been trained. As a matter of fact, this list can actually serve as a tool as you are interviewing project team partners and considering who is best to serve with you in this venture. While our list is not comprehensive, I believe that it will prove to be a useful guide. Each of these items must be considered as you craft your facility master plan.

> **Always plan ahead. It wasn't raining**
> **when Noah built the ark.**
> — Richard Cushing, novelist

Phase I Environmental Study

In the real estate and development industry, this is referred to as a "look-see." According to Wikipedia, it is further defined as "a report prepared for a real estate holding which identifies potential or existing environmental contamination liabilities." The analysis, often called an ESA, typically addresses both the underlying land as well as physical improvements to the property. However, techniques applied in a Phase I ESA never include actual collection of physical samples or chemical analyses of any kind. Scrutiny of the land includes examination of potential soil contamination, groundwater quality, surface water quality, and sometimes issues related to hazardous substance uptake by biota. The examination of a site may include definition of any chemical residues within structures, identification of possible asbestos containing building materials, inventory of hazardous substances stored or used on site, assessment of mold and mildew, and evaluation of other indoor air quality parameters.1 Contaminated sites are often referred to as "brownfield sites." In severe cases, brownfield sites may be added to the National Priorities List where they will be subject to the U.S. Environmental Protection Agency's Superfund program.

Actual sampling of soil, air, groundwater, and building materials is typically not conducted during a Phase I ESA. The Phase I ESA is merely the first step in the process of environmental due diligence. If a site is considered contaminated, a Phase II Environmental Site Assessment may be conducted. This is a more detailed investigation involving chemical analysis for hazardous substances, including petroleum hydrocarbons.

A variety of actions can cause a Phase I study to be performed for a commercial property, which includes a church, even if the land is zoned for residential.2 The most common are:

1. Purchase of real property by a person or entity not previously on title.
2. Contemplation by a new lender to provide a loan on the subject real estate.
3. Application to a public agency for change of use or other discretionary land use permit.

If the Phase I ESA indicates any potential issues, additional assessments will have to be performed.

PHASE II ENVIRONMENTAL SITE ASSESSMENT

This investigation collects original samples of soil, groundwater, or building materials and analyzes them for quantitative values of various contaminants.3 Phase II assessments are normally undertaken when a Phase I ESA determines a likelihood of site contamination.

Rather than assessing environmental impact that has already occurred at a given site, a Phase 1 Environmental Impact Study determines the potential for contamination based on hydrologic features, past usage of the site, and potential hazards such as storage tanks, as well as other risk factors. A "simple" study will generally cost $2,000-$3,000.

PHASE III ENVIRONMENTAL SITE ASSESSMENT

This investigation involves remediation of a site. Phase III investigations aim to delineate the physical extent of contamination based on recommendations made in Phase II assessments. Phase III investigations may involve intensive testing, sampling, and monitoring, as well as "fate and transport" studies and the design of feasibility studies for remediation and remedial plans. This study normally involves assessment of alternative cleanup methods, costs, and logistics. The study report details the steps taken to perform site cleanup and the follow-up monitoring for residual contaminants.

RESEARCH OF DEED RESTRICTIONS

Virtually every deed for a piece of property has some restrictions or restoration covenants. A deed restriction is a legal obligation imposed on a buyer of real estate by the seller. Such restrictions frequently "run with the land" and are enforceable on subsequent buyers of the property.

Deed restrictions, also known as restrictive covenants, are commonly registered against commercial properties. General covenants, such as those restricting the heights of structures or forbidding certain "dirty" businesses (e.g. feedlots or chemical production facilities), are common in areas located near residential communities. Developers may seek to restrict the type of business allowed to operate in a certain area. A purchaser of land in a research park, for example, may not be allowed to construct a bingo parlor or a tool-and-die factory. A commercial property may also include a restrictive covenant forbidding the sale of certain items on the property, such as pornography or liquor.

Residential covenants are relatively common with most deeds. Some residential covenants are fairly straightforward, such as those preventing owners from removing healthy trees, fundamentally altering historically important structures, or directly harming property values. Others, however, are more nuanced. Some restrictive covenants may govern what color a structure's exterior is painted, what and how many exterior decorations are allowed, or where cars may be parked. In working with ministries, I have encountered restrictive covenants that limit the height of steeples, determine maximum land coverage by impervious items, or even allow or disallow the use of the property as a church or other ministry organization. As you develop your master plan and look at physical sites for your facilities, it is important to know of any restrictions and whether or not there are any "go/no go" issues that must be resolved. While many municipalities allow ministry facilities to be located within a residential zoning and classification, the deed restrictions may have conditions that would supersede the actual zoning.

Title Search for Easements, Reservations, Liens, and Other Encumbrances or Limiting Factors

The buyer of a property will usually purchase title insurance, which offers protection from any title problems that may arise after a sale, such as liens that were missed during the title search. The title insurance company submits a report and issues an insurance policy in support of its findings. So what is a title search?

A title search is a process performed primarily to determine the answer to three questions:

1. Can the seller legally sell all or part of the property?
2. What kinds of restrictions or allowances pertain to the use of the land (real covenants, easements, or other servitudes)?
3. Do any liens exist on the property that need to be addressed, such as mortgages, back taxes, mechanics' liens, or other assessments?

Anyone may do a title search and review documents concerning conveyances of land, since these documents are a matter of public record. In most cases, an attorney or a title company does this kind of research, but anyone with the time to do so can gather this information. Title searches are most often carried out before contracting is completed between parties and sometimes during the escrow phase of a closing.

There are several reasons for performing a title search. One may be carried out when an owner of a certain real property wishes to mortgage his property, and the bank requires him to insure the transaction. In the case of a ministry purchasing land, I highly recommend that this search be a contingency to any offer to purchase, and that it be performed as early in the transaction as possible. Even if you already own the property, it would be prudent to do this assessment again. You do not want to invest a great deal of time and money only to find out that there is a restriction that forbids or otherwise negatively affects the work already performed. A title report may show any easements, meaning recorded legal rights, to the property or portions of the property. A previous owner may have legally given a neighbor the right to share the driveway, or the city may have a right to strips of the property for installing power lines, communication lines, water pipes, or sewer pipes. There may also be "reservations" granted to a utility company which give the utility the opportunity to impose the easement at a later time.

A "full coverage search" is usually done when creating a title report for sale/resale transactions and for a transaction that involves construction loans. It generally includes searches related to property liens, easements, covenants, conditions, and restrictions agreements (CC&Rs), as well as resolutions and ordinances that will affect the real property in question.

A common issue discovered during a title search is a lien. A lien is any legal recorded claim against a property. A lien is any legal recorded claim against a property. These encumbrances are placed against real property as a "blemish" requiring payment for a claim by another party. The claim encumbers the property as a means to collect money owed, such as a mortgage, property taxes, or an unpaid debt owed to a contractor who performed work on the property. There are several types of liens you might encounter:

Equitable lien: a property is held as collateral and the parties agree in a document that the property will be used to secure the debt.

General liens: related to real estate and personal property. Court ordered judgments, probate actions, and IRS taxes fall under this category.

Judgment lien: the result of an action by a party or government agency through a court of law to collect payment on a claim.

Involuntary lien: real estate property taxes created by state statutes. These taxes are a claim against the property which the property owner assumes during purchase. Unpaid taxes can result in a specific involuntary lien.

Specific liens: special assessments and mechanics liens. Unpaid contractors from repair and remodeling projects can file a specific lien. Property associations and local governing bodies can issue special assessments for repairs and improvements. Failure to pay these special assessments can result in a lien being placed against a property.

Voluntary lien: mortgages and other voluntary agreements. For example, a mortgage holder may voluntarily agree that the mortgage lien is security for the lender in case of default on the loan.

Liens on ministry property have unique consequences. If you are looking to purchase property, then you need all the liens removed, just as if you were buying property for a house. However, some liens on your existing property, such as the specific liens, may not affect you until you try to sell the property, at which time a buyer would want them all removed. In addition, some states require that a lien be perfected, or a statement of the collateral put on file by the party claiming it. This must be done in order to file a lawsuit against the property owner. The obvious downside of liens on your campus is that they are a matter of public record and can damage your esteem in the community. I strongly recommend that you seek legal counsel regarding any potential or current liens on your current or future real property.

Topography Issues

Topography is generally defined as the detailed mapping or charting of the features of a relatively small area, district, or locality. Additionally, topography includes the detailed description, especially by means of surveying, of particular localities, as cities, towns, or estates, as well as the relief features or surface configurations of an area.

In laymen's terms, this is a surveying process that indicates how the land lies and describes its slopes, inclines, and reliefs. The topography of a site has enormous impact on the cost of development. If you have a steep lot, then you need to consider a project that includes some multi-level structure. If the site is totally flat (which sites rarely are), then you must consider drainage issues. No site is void of topography issues.

Often, topography comes into play when a church feels that it has got an opportunity to purchase land for a price "too good to be true." It is not unheard of for a ministry to purchase land for up to 50% off of market price or appraised value and then have to spend 100% of the value because of challenges related to topography issues.

Sub-surface Investigation

Dirt is dirt, right? As you can imagine, it's not true. All dirt may have been created equally in the book of Genesis, but not all dirt is equal today. As such, it is prudent to do a certain level of sub-surface soil investigation. When you hear terms like soil boring, geotechnical investigation, sampling, soil test, and foundation investigation, you are in the realm of sub-surface investigation.

This investigation reveals whether or not the material under the top soil will be able to support a proposed structure. Just about any site can be built upon, so the issue is how much it will cost to provide the required bearing capacity for the proposed structure. Required remediation can either be accomplished by modifying the soil itself or by modifying the building components. Each can be an acceptable option, with its own set of cost implications.

For example, if you have good soil conditions, you can incorporate a shallow foundation system. But what if the sub-surface soil is not as favorable? You might have to incorporate a number of remedial methodologies. Such systems may include driven pilings, poured pilings, undercut and controlled fill, caissons, and helical piers. Each of these has a significant impact on the rest of the project. The earlier these issues can be determined, the better for projecting cost expectations and making structural modifications. There are few things more discouraging than spending months planning and only then finding out your chosen site has poor soil conditions that will cost you tens or hundreds of thousands of dollars to correct.

Wetlands/Watershed/Flood Plain/Water Table Issues

Water is a powerful natural element. When creating a master plan, it demands your attention. You may already be familiar with the following terms from having discussed property purchases or development of your current property, but let's clarify exactly what each of them describes.

A *wetland* is an area of land whose soil is saturated, at least seasonally and possibly permanently, with moisture. Shallow pools of water may also partially or completely cover such areas. Generally, this "permeated land" is not suitable for development. Federal law also protects wetlands as areas with limited development potential.

A *water table* is the level at which the groundwater pressure is equal to atmospheric pressure. It is essentially the depth at which the first water is found under the surface of the soil. That depth can directly affect development cost, particularly in coastal areas where the ground elevation is relatively close to sea level and thus limits the depth of a structure's foundation.

Watershed, also known as a drainage basin, is an area of land where rainfall or snow-melt drains downhill into a body of water, such as a river, lake, reservoir, estuary, wetland, sea, or ocean. The drainage basin includes not only the streams and rivers that convey the water, but also the land surfaces from which the water drains into those channels.

A *flood plain* is a flat, or nearly flat, area of land adjacent to a stream or river that experiences occasional or periodic flooding. It includes the floodway, which consists of the stream channel and adjacent areas that carry flood flows, and the flood fringes, which are areas covered by the flood, but which do not experience a strong current.

Each of these conditions limit the amount of development that can be performed on a site, and each can have an impact on the cost of development. Understanding water issues is critical when purchasing land and developing both new or existing property. You may need a specialty engineer to make a final determination.

DEAR KING SOLOMON

The majority of this chapter contains some technical stuff, and I'm sure it feels a little cumbersome. So let's take a quick break from technical terms and definitions and look at an example of what might have happened if we had had all of these regulations when Solomon was building the temple. I recently read 1 Kings 6. Take a minute and at least read ^{verses 2-6}. I'll wait on you.

The entire chapter is fascinating to me as a person involved with ministry facility development. But as I started reading those selected verses, I could not avoid letting my mind wander into the realm of the absurd. I started thinking what it would have been like for Solomon if he would have had to get a building permit for the temple based on many of the requirements in modern day code and the topics we are addressing in this chapter. I could not help myself (I am weird that way). The more I thought about it, the more I realized how overwhelming these kind of issues can be to church leaders who just need more space and yet seem to have to deal with a flood of requirements that impact their design, function, and particularly their budget. So what would it have been like for Solomon? The following are some of the things a code official might have confronted the King with had our current codes been enforceable.

Dear King Solomon:

It has come to the building department's attention that you are constructing a new temple for assembly occupancy and public meetings. While we support the development of such structures, we need to bring several critical issues to your attention that require immediate correction and adjustment.

Please read the following and then contact our office with any questions, clarifications, and to provide us with the required documentation. Your prompt compliance with these requirements is appreciated.

1. After searching our files and the scroll room, we are not able to locate an application for a building permit. As a government official, I am sure you

understand the need to adhere to all required rules, regulations, and ordinances. We require a detailed set of plans for our review and approval (please do not submit on stone tablets as we do not have the storage for such).

2. Based on information obtained by our team, it appears that you intend to build the assembly building 90 feet x 30 feet. This would equate to 2,700 square feet. Using our occupancy formula of seven square feet per person, this space could accommodate 385 people (2700/7). The current building code requires all assembly buildings with an occupancy of 300 or more to have an approved automatic fire sprinkler/suppression system. Please ensure that this is reflected in your submitted plans.

3. We understand that you intend to construct the side walls at a height of 45 feet. We have two serious concerns about this. First, please get with the zoning office to ensure that you are in compliance with the height restrictions for that zoning district. Secondly, your project is in a seismic zone that requires special attention given to the structural components of all buildings with special consideration given to builds with such height. Please ensure that your submitted plans address all of these requirements.

4. It is our understanding that you intend to build this structure with three floors. This is of great concern

to us, and we need to draw your attention to our accessibility ordinance. You will need to provide for the vertical accessibility by means of an elevator to reach all three floors. In addition, you will need two other means of fire-rated egress from each floor to a fire-rated exit to the exterior of the building. In addition, please review the ordinance for the required Area of Refuge and the required two-way communication system.

5. Our new building code no longer allows the beams used to support an upper floor to merely rest on the structural wall below. The new code requires the following:

   - Structural footings and pads under all structural loads
   - Columns or other structural accommodation to support upper beams
   - All beams must be mechanically fastened to the columns below using the approved seismic fasteners, hangers, and straps

6. Based on the occupancy calculation above, and our chariot parking requirement of one space per four seats, you will need to provide 97 parking spaces (385/4) which must include the appropriate ratio of handicap enabled spaces.

We believe there will be more items to address once we receive and review your signed and sealed building plans. However, these are critical items that must be addressed before you submit.

Thanks you for your understanding and prompt attention to these matters.

As always, please remember that we are the government and are here to "help."

Sincerely,

Mr. Building Official

SETBACKS AND RIGHT-OF-WAYS

In land development, a *setback* is the distance that a building, parking lot, or other structure is removed from a street or road, another property, a river or other stream, a shore or flood plain, or any other place that needs protection. Setbacks are generally set by municipal ordinances and can be found by doing research with the local zoning office or building official. (One side note: If the details of roadway setbacks are not incorporated in the zoning ordinances, you may have to contact the Department of Transportation for clarification.)

A *right-of-way* describes the right of a non-owning party or the public at large to traverse a piece of land. The term also refers to the land subject to such a right. Generally, there is a predetermined manner or route of travel over the land. An easement is an example of a right-of-way. A public right-of-way permits public travel, such as a street, road, sidewalk, or footpath. Sometimes, a right-of-way may refer to a utility easement, such as a power line.

These restrictions will affect the amount of land usable for development. In most cases you cannot build, park on, or otherwise develop within these areas. In fact, in many municipalities, you will have a yard or street setback accompanied by a buffer zone, which, in essence, means you have two setback areas limiting the development area.

Tree and Landscape Issues

"What do you mean we can't cut down our trees?" Surprisingly, in most municipalities you cannot cut down trees or clear the land without a land disturbance permit. In fact, in some areas, you cannot cut down "landmark" or "heritage" trees at all. At the least, you cannot remove them without a public hearing and formal approval. Some areas may have a recompense process, which means that you must replace every tree removed with another tree of a designated species and of a specific diameter (typically determined by caliper inch), while others impose a fee for each tree that is removed. All of these issues will affect your development process and costs. I recommended that you obtain a tree survey at the same time that you obtain the boundary and topography survey. A tree survey will identify the location, size, and species of all of your site's trees that measure above a specified minimum diameter.

Landscaping also has a significant impact on most projects. Virtually every municipality has some level of requirement for landscaping. Landscape buffers are common and affect not only the developable area but also the cost to the project. Have your team research and understand the zoning ordinances for landscape buffers, entrance ways, right-of-way landscape requirements, roadway landscaping, and any other requirements they might find on the books.

Many zoning ordinances will have buffer exceptions that allow a hybrid approach to the landscape buffer through some combination of fencing and denser landscape material. You may want to exceed the minimum requirements, however, merely for the benefit of the aesthetics of the campus. The appearance of your campus makes the first impression on the community and your guests, and that first impression will shape their perception of the kind of ministry and neighbor you are and will be in the future.

BUILDING CODES, ACCESSIBILITY CODES, FIRE PROTECTION, AND MORE

There are many different groups and people who will serve as the *authority having jurisdiction* (AHJ) over any land or building development or expansion. Some are state regulated, while others are governed by a county, city, township, province, or municipality. There are also some codes and governing bodies that have national acceptance, which is then interpreted and enforced on a local or state level. The International Code Council has attempted to unify building codes by developing *The International Building Code (IBC)*.

Many states have adopted portions of the IBC. Others have customized the IBC by adding amendments. To further complicate the situation, not every state or municipality uses the same edition of the IBC, of which there are now over six iterations. As you can imagine, this often creates immense confusion!

Here's an example of how the same code (IBC) has been modified in the adjacent states of North and South Carolina. The IBC, in its native form, requires that you provide an automatic fire sprinkler system for any "assembly occupancy" (which describes a worship space, fellowship space, or even a multipurpose space) that can accommodate three hundred people or more. There are two ways to determine occupancy. If you have fixed seating (seats that are bolted or otherwise affixed to the floor), you can use a measurement of eighteen inches per seat. This eighteen-inch rule applies to pews and other forms of bench seating. But if you are going to utilize moveable seating (stacked or folding chairs), then occupancy is calculated by determining the square footage of the assembly space and dividing it by seven square feet per person.

Seating Capacity
(For "flexible" or movable seating) Total square feet of assembly room divided by seven square feet per person equals allowable people.

EXAMPLE:
2,100 SF / 7 SF per person = **300 people**

Therefore, if you have an assembly space that is 2,100 square feet or larger, and you intend to use flexible seating, you must have a fire sprinkler. The state of South Carolina holds to this interpretation of the code tightly. If you are a church in South Carolina and you intend to build any space that could be deemed an assembly occupancy with flexible seating, then any room over 2,100 square feet will need to be equipped with an automatic sprinkler system. Tough requirement, right? That's what

South Carolina's neighbor state thought. So North Carolina added amendments to the IBC. In North Carolina, it is only necessary to install a fire sprinkler system in a room of 12,000 square feet if it is being used for a place of worship. If you are located in North Carolina and want to build an assembly-occupancy facility with flexible seating, you can build a room that can accommodate 1,000 people before you are required to install sprinklers. This results in a huge difference in factors that churches in North and South Carolina must consider. You must know which code applies to your location and project. You must understand how it affects your project. And have your team conduct a detailed code analysis as you get started.

DOT ISSUES

The DOT (Department of Transportation) can influence your master plan and project development in many ways. The following is a partial list of items you will need to take into consideration.

Curb Cuts. Can you add a driveway from your site to the adjoining road(s)? If so, how many and how far apart must they be?

Traffic Counts. Many metropolitan areas require that you retain a firm to perform a traffic impact study to include traffic counts. This data, in concert with the municipalities' projection of the number of vehicles that your developed property will add to the traffic count, determines the total projected traffic on those roadways. Many of these major roadways have designated "trip counts," codifying how many cars per day can have access to the roadway. If the projected count of new vehicles plus the existing traffic count exceeds the total trip counts, your project could be in jeopardy. I have been involved with some projects where the DOT or local municipality required the church to buy additional trip counts, which is essentially a DOT "tax" on organizations that helps to pay for road improvements.

Acceleration and Deceleration Lanes. The municipality or DOT may mandate acceleration and/or deceleration lanes to provide for the safe access to the developed property. They may also require special signage or traffic signals. Factors such as the number of lanes, the speed limit, and the traffic impact play a role in to all of these decisions.

SITE UTILITY AVAILABILITY

Site utilities have always been an issue for any development or expansion project, but with the adoption of the IBC, it becomes even more critical to consider them. One of the most noteworthy changes that the IBC brought was the requirement of fire sprinkler systems in buildings coded for assembly occupancy.

At first, this may not seem like a big deal. You'll just install a sprinkler system if you need to, right? Sure, as long as you have a water supply. Do you have public water available? If so, does it have ample pressure to fight a fire? There are several alternate methods to provide the water supply, but none of them is economical. Water towers, water tanks, and monitored ponds are all usable options, if your local fire marshal agrees, but each is an expensive proposition. I have built ponds to accommodate sprinkler requirements that cost the project close to $250,000 extra—a huge chunk of money to spend for a trustworthy system you pray you will never need to utilize.

Let's talk about it in ministry terms. If you did not have to build that kind of water supply, how much more ministry space could you build? If we assume that you could build added space for $150 per square foot, then you could build another 1,700 square feet. If you are considering worship space, this equates to another one hundred seats or more. I trust that you are beginning to see that seemingly "technical" issues can have real kingdom implications!

> **Planning is bringing the future into the present
> so that you can do something about it now.**
> — Alan Lakein, writer

Other utilities you need to consider include the public sewer, electric service, and gas lines. Your project team should contact the local utilities early in the planning process to make sure they understand all the requirements and implications of these areas.

LOCAL REVIEW BOARD

In addition to written codes, many municipalities have local review boards, Development Review Committees, Architectural Review Boards, and the like. I have found that coastal areas (like those in Florida and California) and resort areas are the most likely to have such public review processes. If you went to develop a property in Miami, you might have to spend between one and three years in the Development Review Committee (DRC) process *before* you can even submit for a building permit. I am seeing this level of scrutiny becoming more and more commonplace across the country.

It behooves you to find out as far in advance as possible if you will have to undergo a review, so that you can address the requisite processes and requirements. Your project team should do the due diligence to determine what other groups and organizations have influence on your project. They will need to obtain and note the dates when the groups meet so they can ensure they follow the process for submitting documents in a timely fashion. It is not uncommon for these public groups, generally comprising volunteers from the community, to meet only once a month. In order to afford them enough time to review the relevant documentation, they generally require you to submit your application package to them the month prior to the meeting at which you desire to be on the docket.

Remember, even if you follow all the rules and regulations, your project may not be approved. What if it does not pass the first time? Don't panic. You can resubmit. Of course, the same timing holds for resubmission of your application package. As a result, you could be adding in months you did not originally budget just to get the approval you need to move ahead. The clock is ticking, and if you have not planned accordingly for this part of the process, you could be delaying the project, which may in turn affect the interest rate on your loan and the cost of materials and labor.

Variances and Special Use Permits

A *variance* is an official permit to do something forbidden by regulations, especially by building in a way or for a purpose normally forbidden by a zoning law or building code. For example, imagine a zoning ordinance that limits the height of a building to thirty feet above grade, but you have designed a building that is thirty-two feet tall. You can petition a variance for the additional two feet. Perhaps the zoning ordinance requires two hundred paved parking spaces for your project, but you do not have enough land to provide all of those spaces. You can petition a variance either to reduce the parking requirements or to allow for a certain amount of parking spaces to be located off-site.

The most common variance requests are associated with parking, building height, or setbacks. The ease of getting approval from the local authority having jurisdiction, however, is as varied as the numbers of municipalities in the country. Therefore, it pays to do some due diligence before you start this process.

It is strongly recommended that any person considering seeking a Special Use Permit first contact their local zoning office, which can explain the particular review process, applicable requirements and standards, potential issues, and provide the necessary forms and checklists.

A *special use permit* allows a specific exception to the zoning regulations. The exception must come from a list of acceptable exceptions for a particular parcel of land in a district of a particular zoning character. The local zoning authority reviews and grants special use permits.

Land use is governed by a set of regulations generally known as ordinances or municipal codes, which are authorized by the state's zoning enabling law. Within an ordinance is a list of land-use designations, commonly known as *zoning*. Each different type of zone has its own set of allowed, or *by-right* uses, and extra, or special uses that require obtaining a special use permit before building. Many times, a church will want to build in a residential area not zoned for church facilities. In order to move forward even a step, a special use permit is required.

Acquiring a special use permit represents yet another extra step that you may have to take to receive approval to build. Usually a planning commission or other legislative body must hold a public hearing in order to grant special use permits. This can introduce an unfortunate element of politics to the decision-making process, which may negatively affect your project.

WATER DETENTION AND RETENTION ISSUES

Most jurisdictions require that a developed parcel of land not produce any more storm water run-off than it would have if it were undeveloped. At some point in your design process you will need to engage a civil engineer to perform a hydrology study (the study of the movement, distribution, and quality of water). While you do not need the hydrology study in the earliest phases of your process, you should recognize that detention and retention will need to be addressed on your site and in your master plan.

Water detention can be addressed in several ways. The development of out-fill ditches, swales, and other natural elements have the least impact on the site by taking advantage of its natural features, and are thus usually the least costly. Other means to retain and detain storm water include detention ponds, storm drainage systems, and underground retention systems.

More jurisdictions are becoming sensitive to storm

water run-off, which makes this issue significant in your planning. If it is not an option to make use of swales, out-fill ditches, or other natural aspects of the property, then detention ponds are generally the most cost-effective, particularly if your topography will allow for gravity to bring about "sheet flowing" of the storm water to the pond. If that is not the case, then you may be able to install a system of pipes to accomplish the same net result, but at a higher development cost. Many municipalities also have storm-water systems that are placed under public streets and right-of-ways. If such systems are available, you should explore the possibility of utilizing these resources.

Parking Issues—Ratios, Pervious vs. Impervious, and More Parking lots and vehicular access on your site will most likely consume the largest physical area of any part of your project. On average, you can obtain ninety to a hundred parking spaces per acre of usable land, assuming the land is relatively level.

Virtually every municipality has a zoning ordinance that includes a section concerning parking requirements. Generally for a church, ministry facility, or assembly space, the ratios are based on a certain number of seats in your largest assembly space for every parking space. I have seen these ratios range from three to five seats per parking space.

Given that the total number of seats is calculated based on the type of seating you select, I recommend that you do a parking count to establish your own real-world ratio over three to four weeks. Have a designated person count the number of cars you have on- and off-site during your worship service. From this data you will be able to determine your own parking ratio. I have found that most ministries need one space for every two to two-and-a-half seats. This can fall below a 2:1 ratio if you have a lot of families with teenagers or have multiple services.

Perform your own **Parking Ratio Study**. It is easy! Using a simple formula you can determine your own parking requirements. Assign a designated person or team to do an audit of cars parked in your parking lots, as well as off-site or on-street.

Then determine your attendance during that service and divide the attendance by the number of cars parked. This will give you the ratio.

EXAMPLE:

500 people / 250 cars = **2:1**

Let's see how this might play out. Take our earlier example of the church with three hundred seats. Let's assume the local code has a three-to-one ratio (three seats per parking space). In this scenario you would need one hundred parking spaces (three hundred seats divided by three seats per space). That translates to between one and 1.5 acres just for parking to meet "code minimum."

That's all well and good, but what if your specific ministry needs a 2:1 ratio? In that case you need 150 spaces (three hundred seats at a 2:1 ratio). This means you will need between 1.5 and 2 acres just for parking. As you can see, the available land can be chewed up quickly. If you consider that the building in this scenario could be 10,000 and 15,000 square feet (or up to a third of an acre) you will need over two acres of usable and developable land just for your building and parking. Then you need to add land for the setbacks, buffers, detention and retention, green areas, and growth potential. Most churches underestimate the amount of total land they will need.

In addition to the land mass of the parking areas, you must consider what materials these areas will comprise. The most common is asphalt (black top) and most metropolitan jurisdictions require this as well. However, asphalt is an impervious material, meaning water will not pass through it. The more impervious material you have, the larger your detention and retention areas must be. Deciding on the surface covering of your parking areas early in the process will help the team determine the potential size of your detention area.

If you are in an area that allows for pervious parking surfaces, such as gravel or grass, you may want to consider these options. They can reduce the initial cost of your parking area, as well as reduce the impact of impervious parking. I have worked in coastal regions that actually prefer pervious parking in order to lessen the impacts of storm water runoff.

This chapter has been full of technical detail, hasn't it? I trust you are not overwhelmed or discouraged. Just remember, if you are the key ministry leader, your job is not to master every technical detail, but rather to gather the right team of people who have the expertise needed, excite them with kingdom vision, equip them, and let them serve and lead!

CHAPTER FIVE:
THE RIGHT TOOL—
THE FACILITY MASTER
PLAN, PART B

Plans are worthless. Planning is essential."
— President Dwight D. Eisenhower

At this point in the master-planning process, you have a lot of data at your disposal. It's time to move to the next step: carefully analyzing the data so that you can put the right tool in place for ministry. Did you notice I did not mention the building in the previous sentence? That was deliberate. Much of what we considered in the previous chapter focused on building code issues, regulations, and physical components of a potential project. However, now I am talking about a tool and not a building. Why?

Based on an informal survey, I polled several leaders in the church world and asked a simple question: "How many churches meet in a facility?" My panel of experts did not know of a formal study answering this question. So, the panel made some assumptions, and they surmise that at least 95-99% meet in a facility. That might be a church building, a retail center, office building, school, tattoo parlor, bar, community center . . . or even a house. Here is reality: The overwhelming majority of North American churches in the 21st century use some form of built environment to serve as shelter for their gatherings.

The problem with that paradigm is far too often we assume that a "building" is the right solution for every ministry initiative or perceived spatial concern. I am not convinced. I realize it sounds counterintuitive from a guy who has provided for his family for the majority of his adult life developing church facilities, but that is where my heart and head reside. That is why I believe you have to start with the Ministry Master Plan as the basis for *every* evaluation related to future planning

Before the pretty picture of your kingdom vision can be put in the frame, you'll need to go through three areas of analysis:

- Site Feasibility
- Space Allocation and Program Study
- Facility Audit (for churches with existing structures)

Each of these areas of analysis will have a significant impact on your master plan.

SITE FEASIBILITY

You have just collected a *ton* of data related to your site. You and your project team know which codes apply, what your soil conditions are, and whether or not you have wetlands to navigate. Now, what do you do with all of this data? The team needs to develop a project site analysis report that will focus on the following criteria:

- How much usable land mass is available for our project? Once all of the setbacks, buffers, easements, and right-of-ways have been identified, what is left? How much can be developed?

- Do we have certainty about intersections or other off-site conditions that should be accounted for, such as road medians, signal lights, and cross roads?

- What are the parking criteria and how much land mass will that require? Remember to explore not only what the jurisdiction will require, but also what your specific ministry will demand.

- What topography issues do we face, and how do they change the usable land mass and the placement of structures? Do we need to consider a basement or multistory structure? Do we need to address tiered parking?

- What zoning and public/private issues need to be addressed? What are the timelines and deliverables for each? Can we build what we want with the current zoning, or do we need to obtain a special use permit? If so, how long will that take, and how far into the process can we get before it becomes a "go/no-go" issue?

- Will any variances be required for the plan? Are there any issues that could affect the height, parking, or other parameters of our building project?
- What utilities are available? How will their availability (or lack thereof) impact our usable land mass?
- Is water and sewer available to our site, and are they of adequate size?
- Do we have any deed or title issues to be addressed or avoided? If so, are any of them deal-breakers?
- Are there any other reports or tests that need to be performed on the site? Will the bank require a Phase I ESA?

With this list and the subsequent analysis in hand, you will have a good foundation from which to understand the physical constraints of the property. This baseline will help the project team make recommendations in light of the physical attributes of your property, uncover any issues those attributes create, and choose next steps.

Space Allocation and Program Study

This next step is a combination of two processes: space allocation of existing structures (if any), and programmatic study of desired and/or needed space.

If your ministry has existing structures that you intend to continue to use, then you will need to conduct a space allocation study. It is important to do a room-by-room evaluation of all your space to determine the following:

- Size of the room
- Current use and by what groups
- What days the space is used by said groups
- How many are in attendance at each use
- Are there any untouchable "sacred cows" (say it isn't so)?
- How many times the room "turns" in a week or a day (set up, tear down, and re-set up)

This step clarifies whether or not your existing space is being used in the most effective way. More than once, I have seen this step result in a church determining that it needs to build less new space and hence spend less money!

The primary design tool in facility master planning process is the Program Study, and it involves several steps. The first step is "discovery," which is often the first time that ministry leaders get down to the nuts and bolts of daily ministry realities.

For example, we might consider the children of our ministry. How many kids are in the nursery now? What is our ratio of children to adults? Do we expect that to change as the ministry grows? Those are just a few questions, and just related to the children's needs. The leadership must take a clear-eyed, honest look at dozens of questions like these.

This discovery process can include as many leaders as you deem appropriate. The most important thing is to have a good cross-section of people. If the stakeholders involved in this process are all involved in the worship ministry, you would find that their priorities would revolve around the size of the platform, the acoustics, the amount of lighting, the greenroom space, and so on. They may not understand the details pertinent to the children's space or to the gathering area.

After discovery, you must hold a debriefing with the ministry's senior leadership. This debriefing will allow the senior leadership to hear directly from those involved in discovery, as well as to ensure that the desires and needs of the individual ministry leaders are in tune with the overall vision of the church as a whole. If you find that your individual leaders are getting off base or chasing endeavors inconsistent with the vision, you must work to achieve unity of purpose before you get much further down the road in the master planning process.

Now, it is time to add a narrative element to your study,

bringing facts together with dreams. If we plan for X kids in the nursery, then at Y square feet per child, we will need Z square feet. In addition, we want a private toilet room for each classroom. We also want lockable storage closets and shelving in each room.

Children Space Planning Example
CLASSROOM:
40 children (toddlers) @ 35 SF/child =1,400 SF
TOILET ROOM: Minimum of 25 SF
STORAGE CLOSET: Suggested size of 25 SF
TOTAL: 1,450 SF

This process should be completed for every ministry area with the guidance and leadership of your project team members (don't try to do this alone). At the completion of these discussions, you should have a net usable square footage number. Then you need to account for common areas, such as restrooms, corridors, an electrical room, a sprinkler room, mechanical room(s), storage areas, and wall thickness. These items will add a "grossing factor" that can easily increase the building size 15-25% over the net usable square feet.

For example, your team may have determined that you need 20,000 square feet of usable square footage.

We now need to accommodate the ancillary spaces mentioned above. If we assume that you need a grossing factor of 20%, this will increase your total square footage needs to 24,000 square feet. When determining gross square footage (which is the most common measurement when discussing the total square footage of a building), remember to measure from the outside faces of the building. Any other methodology for measuring will give you a false sense of the actual size of the overall structure.

FACILITY AUDIT

This step will help you determine if your existing physical structures are compatible with your long range plan or if you will need to make radical changes to your current infrastructure. This is different than the space allocation study mentioned earlier. I recommend conducting a two-part evaluation, involving both a physical and a functional analysis.

The *physical analysis* addresses all the elements of the primary structural system (what holds the building up and together), the secondary structural elements (what you see and what keeps the weather out), the service systems (mechanical, electrical and plumbing), and the safety standards.

- Is the structure generally sound?

- Are the heating and ventilation systems adequate?
- What is the condition of the wiring? The plumbing?
- Are the floors solid and level? Will they hold their intended weight loads?
- What is the practical, useful life expectancy of the facility?
- How much are operating costs?
- Are there preventive maintenance schedules and related budget resources in place?
- If significant buildings and grounds investments are required, what are the economics of the situation?
- Is the roof in good condition? Does it drain well?
- Does the structure meet building codes? Is it worth keeping? Can it be renovated or modified? Should it be?

The *functional analysis* evaluates how well the building fulfills its current intended purpose, and how it will fulfill its purpose in the long term. It also determines how accessible the building is for those with various handicaps, especially those prevalent among an aging population.

- Are users of the facility crowded, or is there wasted space? What is the ratio of non-usable to usable space?
- Does the facility have historical significance? Is it significant in terms of your heritage? Would it have value to someone else?
- Is the property conveniently located for other development?

- Does the facility meet your program needs?
- Does the building offer operational efficiencies? Could it?
- Does the facility "fit" in the context of the overall property and community?
- Is it congruent with our "story?"
- Is this the highest and best use of the site and facilities?
- Do adjacent spaces make sense for how we want to use the facility? Can this be changed?
- Are there challenges with the Americans with Disability Act and access issues?
- Will it comply with current building codes and ordinances?
- Does the facility deliver your image and positioning in the market and to your target?
- Does the facility support your mission/purpose/vision?

With this analysis complete, the moment of reckoning is upon us: *Does the financial analysis reconcile with the functional analysis?*

What do you do if your financial spreadsheet indicates you can afford 20,000 square feet but your program study reflects you desire for 50,000 square feet? This is where the leadership must meet its greatest challenge, as you must negotiate among those passionately committed—and rightfully so—to their own ministry areas. Every ministry leader believes that he or she must have all of the space indicated on the program study. No one can give up an inch.

How do you move ahead? I suggest three steps. First, remind all leaders of the mission, vision, target, story, and DNA of your church to ensure that everyone is in lockstep agreement, not just intellectually, but with heart and soul. Next, review your facts and your faith. You made some key decisions during the process of understanding that dynamic tension. Finally, resist the urge to talk about "cutting" ministries or plans. It is much more helpful to talk of intentionally phasing certain aspects over the course of the project, as time and finances permit.

These discussions will be challenging, perhaps even emotional. But in the strongest possible terms I urge you to have them at this point in the process. The short-term pain may well result in increased clarity, unity, and intentionality. This is the critical point were "blue-sky" thinking must shift to intentional planning. By doing so, you will avoid the long-term pain of demoralized leaders and financial peril if you are deliberate in this phase. Now we move to the final component of master planning: making sure your facility is sustainable.

CHAPTER SIX:
LIFE CYCLE, FACILITY STEWARDSHIP, AND LONGEVITY—SUSTAINING MASTER PLANS

The process had not always been a smooth one but, six months later, the project team had reached a remarkable degree of unity. Together they had gained true insight into First Church's financial realities, ministry vision, DNA, story, and target. They had prioritized the most important goals for the next stretch of years, and they had arrived at a common understanding of their physical plant needs. Most important, there was a sense of possibility, of enthusiasm, and of hope.

In a few moments, the design professional would offer the big reveal of the pretty pictures Bob had wanted for so long. Meeting with Tom in the pastor's office moments before the meeting began, Bob had glanced again at the drawings and paused to thank God for his faithfulness, guidance, and patience.

"You know," he mused to Tom and to the architect as

they walked together down the hallway to the conference room, "I had no idea what was going to be involved in this process when I began it. When I found out . . . well, let's just say that there have been more than a few moments I have wanted to bail completely." He laughed and shook his head.

"But to tell you the truth, I have never been more excited about ministry and about the future of a church than I am right now. I really believe that by God's grace, First Church's greatest days are ahead of her."

Pastor Bob smiled at his new friends and opened the door to the conference room.

ஐભ

The fourth master plan is one that most churches fail to consider, even though it is the most costly stage in the life cycle of any facility. In most circles, the term "life cycle" is related to the longevity or life expectancy of a physical element, such as our ministry facilities we discussed in the previous chapter. It is also used in referring to processes, systems, and research.

While I believe that understanding and developing proactive initiatives is a critical component of the master planning process, we may be better served to think of a term that is more encompassing than simply a life cycle. The word *sustaining* is a better word to describe the real need and meaning of the fourth master plan. Let's look at how the dictionary describes both terms:

Life Cycle: a series of stages through which something (as an individual, culture, or manufactured product) passes during its lifetime

Sustaining: to provide what is needed for something or someone to exist and to continue to exist.

The above definition of life cycle would imply a specific duration or "lifetime." Something that has a prescribed timeframe for its existence and function. Sustaining, on the other hand, carries the meaning of continuance, without an end in mind. I believe that for our discussion, both concepts are needed and, in fact, mandatory.

In the same way that there are multiple master plans, this master planning process has multiple components and application. Each part is critical to the longevity and viability of each of the others. To neglect these evaluations and plans would render the initial master plans irrelevant and shortsighted. The previous three master plans are forward thinking. We plan our ministries, then the finances, and then the facilities. These are things we can dream about. We can envision them. Our project team can draw pretty pictures, and we can virtually walkthrough the conceived structures. These plans jump right to the forefront of our thinking just like the initial steps of planning our vacation.

But where the vacation analogy loses some relevance

is related to this fourth and most critical component when we look at the long term. We must consider the sustainability of each of the three more tangible plans. Without forethought and planning for the life cycle and long-term implications, we will have only considered the here and now and possibly burdened future leaders and even generations with flash-in-the-pan concepts. Obviously, your current leadership does not want to leave the next generation with a financial unstable infrastructures that has costly money pits.

Let's start this exploration of the Sustaining Master Plan with the most obvious—facilities. This is the opposite order of the initial processes, but in many ways can be the most costly to your ministry. Additionally, facility stewardship is the one that is rarely considered when we are in the dreaming phase of our planning.

FACILITY STEWARDSHIP

As we have explored in the previous chapters, it would be foolish to develop a plan for physical facilities that did not meet your ministry vision. I doubt any church would knowingly enter into a plan that is financially unattainable. It's also a travesty to spend millions of kingdom dollars on facilities, only to have no idea how to steward them well. Yet the common approach is to start drawing pretty pictures and bubble diagrams on a site plan without much if any thought as to the long-term care of the shiny new facilities. What is needed is what I call "facility stewardship." For some of you this may be a new concept. You know what a facility is, and you are probably familiar with stewardship. But how do the two go together? Let's first look at the definition of each:

Facility: Something designed, built, or installed to serve a specific function for a convenience or service.

Stewardship: The act of being a steward. A person who manages another's property or financial affairs; one who administers anything as the agent of another.

If you have grown up in the church or been involved in church for any period of time, you have probably heard the term "stewardship." I am sure that in almost every case, it revolved around money or raising money. In these cases, we are generally talking about financial stewardship, which is a critical element of our spiritual life, as well as the life of our ministries.

The word "money" is used over 140 times in scripture, and if you add terms such as "gold" and "silver" the number is even higher. For example, words and phrases revolving around financial matters are mentioned more often in the Bible than prayer, healing, and mercy. But stewardship is not just about money and finances. It refers to (as its definition above indicates) the caring for or oversight of something which is someone else's.

To gain a better understanding, let's first look at the principle of *entrusted vs. entitled*. I believe that God has entrusted us with the stewarding of all of these items. For me, I believe that stewardship is less about what we *give* and more about taking care of what we have been *given*. So, how do we define *entrusted*? According to dictionary. com, it can be defined as follows.

Entrust: to charge or invest with a trust or responsibility; to commit (something) in trust to; confide, as for care, use, or performance.

What does that mean to you? To me, it means that when something (or someone) is entruted to me, I am responsible to care for it, to be in charge of it, and to be responsible for it. That sounds a lot like stewardship.

I am burdened by the millions—indeed billions—of dollars that are spent each year on religious construction without a clear understanding of the "real" cost of ownership. Did you realize that there is about $5-6 billion spent on religious construction every year? I believe that most ministry leaders do not have a complete understand that the ongoing costs of a facility eclipse the initial costs and do so in a much bigger way than you would imagine.

The cost of owning a facility is not merely the cost to get it built. That is only the tip of the iceberg. It is, unfortunately, the primary aspect that most people fixate on. It is the first thing church leaders contemplate when they consider a facility initiative. "What will it cost?" However, that initial cost is only one facet of the total cost of facility stewardship.

Facility Stewardship encompasses all aspect of the cost of owning a facility . . . and not just the initial cost of sticks and bricks. Many churches have to leverage their project by borrowing monies. So, you will have the "cost of money" (interest paid to a lender). There is also operational costs. These set of costs are the ones that blindside most churches as they are the largest component of facility ownership and are the only element that is not finite. These costs are virtually perpetual. As long as you own the facility, you will pay utility bills. You will have paper products to purchase and light bulbs to replace.

With that as a foundation, let's look at the *real* cost of stewarding a ministry facility, taking into account each aspect of facility stewardship costs:

1. *Initial Cost:* For this exercise, let's assume that our new ministry facility is 30,000 square feet and we can have it built for $145 per square feet. Of that, the construction partner's fee was 6%, and we paid the design professional a fee of 7% of the construction value. We will also assume that the land has been paid for and is unencumbered of debt. So what do the numbers look like?

   INITIAL COST: 30,000 SF x $145/SF = $4,3500,000 plus design fees = $4,654,500

2. *Cost of Money:* Let's assume that we borrowed

$3,000,000 to pay for the project and we did so based on a 15-year loan at 6%. Let's also assume the loan was paid off in seven years. In this scenario, you will have paid approximately $1.1 million in interest.

3. *Cost of Operation:* Based on our research and benchmarking provided by IFMA (International Facility Managers Association), the average church in America will spend $5.50 to $7.50 per square foot annually for janitorial services, utilities and general maintenance. In addition, a church will spend an additional amount in capital improvements that will be in the $1.00 to $2.00 per square foot range. For the sake of this exercise, let's assume that we will spend $7.00 per square foot for operational and capital reserve items. This may be low, but we want the calculations to be realistic. I was recently contacted by an Atlanta-based design professional who shared that in 2010 the Building Owners and Managers Association also used $6.50 to $7.00 per square foot as their bench mark number.

30,000 SF x $7.00/SF = $210,000/year.

Assume a 40-year life cycle (which is not that long) at 1.5% per year of inflation. Remember, that operational costs are perpetual and paid for with inflated dollars, so this is going to increase. And 1.5% is probably *too low*.

$210,000/ year x 40 years = $8,400,000 + 60% (1.5% per year inflation for 40 years . . . without compounding) = $13,440,000

So let's look at what this means:

1. Initial costs including design: $4,654,500
2. Cost of money: $1,100,000
3. Cost of life cycle operations and capital reserve: $13,440,000 (that is $448 per square foot!)

The total cost of ownership is $19,194,500. That is certainly a large number. But here is the shocking part:

1. The combined cost of the construction partner and the design professionals is only 3% of the total cost of ownership
2. The construction cost, including the design, is only about 23% of the total cost of ownership.
3. The interest paid is only about 6% of the total cost of ownership
4. Which leaves a whopping 71% of the total cost of ownership in operation costs and capital expenditures.

In a similar study, State Farm Insurance found that they spend about 80% of the total cost of ownership of commercial buildings on operational costs over 40 year. Further, a book was published in 1969 by The American Institute of Architects and written by David S. Haviland reveals the following insight:

"The initial design and construction of a facility comprises about 15% of the total cost of a building over its 40 year lifespan. The remaining 85% is made up of the building's operations and maintenance costs."

These numbers clearly indicate that the costs *after* you occupy the building far exceed actually building the facility. So, do we invest the same amount of time and energy in planning our operational costs as we do developing our physical master plans? Might too much be made of architect and construction partner fees? The fees that encompass only 3% of the total cost of ownership feel so important at the time we hire these professionals, but the decisions, direction, means, and methods that this team suggests and implements will be with you for the life of your buildings. Do we have our eyes on the *real* cost of facility ownership?

If facility stewardship is really about being wise stewards of all God has entrusted, then I think it is fair to say that most of us have our priorities upside down. Facility stewardship must include proactive facility management and long-term care.

THE REST OF THE SUSTAINING STORY

The balance of the sustaining master plan becomes a little but more convoluted, but it is important. This part involves the systems, processes, and philosophies that must be developed and reviewed continuously to ensure that the ministry and financial master plans are also sustainable. The facility stewardship component is more closely related to our definition of life cycle. Physical components of any built environment have a point in their life where they no longer can exist and perform the function they were intended to. All of your carpet at some time will have to be replaced. It has a fairly specific life expectancy. The same applies for your roof material and HVAC systems. It is true that you can do some things to extend that life, but you cannot cause it to continue to function with the same efficiency as originally designed.

On the other hand, our ministry and financial master plans are far more organic, and thus sustainable. They are going to morph and evolve. They shift with culture and other internal and external influencers. Demographics, recessions, and politics can all impact the vibrancy of a ministry. I believe that some churches have a life cycle as well, but most are sustainable if they are intentional about being so.

Unlike facility stewardship, the sustaining master plan related to finances and ministry initiatives are less concrete. There are not prescriptive lists that you can assign to a facility manager to check the box to know things have been done and then follow a spreadsheet to know when the next major milestone will occur like you do when replacing the filters in your HVAC equipment. However, there are deliberate steps that can be implemented to keep the sustaining process at the forefront of your leadership team's mind.

When you occupy your new or newly renovated facility, one of the first action items the church should take is establishing your operations budget, means, and methods. There are a number of things that should be incorporated into your systems that are best practices. Some of the most basic items are things like:

- Schedule for changing HVAC filters
- Regular inspections of your fire extinguishers
- Painting plans for keeping the facility looking fresh
- Grounds maintenance plans and schedule
- Capital reserve planning
- Floor finish replacement schedule
- Carpet extraction plan

Other items that should be incorporated include an annual financial audit by an outside firm that can provide you with markers, indicators, and early warning signs of things to note. The same would apply to having an ongoing and proactive generosity plan to lead your congregation in the theology of biblical giving. That coupled with your finance team performing periodic financial evaluations and benchmarking are all key components to staying on top of your financial master plan and making the needed adjustments and alignments as deemed appropriate. Remember what we said in the first chapter? A master plan, even financial, is a snapshot of the future we believe God has called us to fulfill based on current information.

THE REST OF THE STORY
FOR PASTOR BOB

Dedication of the new facility was a tremendous event. There were local and state dignitaries in attendance as well as family, friends, and even some of Pastor Bob's predecessors. The weather was perfect and the excitement was palpable.

"We did it," Pastor Bob whispered to himself. Walking up to shake Tom's had, Pastor Bob said in an excited voice, "Hey Tom, isn't it great that the project is done? Now we can focus on ministry. No more worry about the facilities!"

Tom starred at his pastor as if he had lost his mind. "Do you really think our work is done?" asked Tom.

"Sure. We are in this new facility and the heavy lifting is over. We are ready to rock and roll!"

Tom paused and then asked, "Remember when you bought your new car a few months ago?" Pastor Bob nodded fondly. He loves his new car. Tom continued, "Do you remember the owner's manual the dealer gave you? Was there any information about maintaining the car?"

"Yeah, but what does that have to do with our new building?" Bob asked a little confused.

Tom continues, "Did they tell you how often you need to change the oil or rotate the tires? Did they suggest that you bring it after so many miles? Did they talk to you about replacing the timing belt? I am sure that you would not drive your car for more than 5,000 miles without changing the oil and filter.

If we are that conscious about an asset that will only last 5-10 years, how much more diligence and intentionality will be required to steward an asset that could last 50-100 years?"

"I had never thought about it that way Tom," Pastor Bob admitted. "I just assumed that once we moved in that we could take our attention off the facility and it would sort of 'take care of itself' without much effort on our part."

Bob continued, "I want to be a good steward of what God has entrusted to us. We need to get the team back together to make sure we have the right plans in place to manage and care for this incredible asset God has blessed us with."

"Agreed," said Tom. "We need to be proactive and not allow our facility to become an albatross around the necks of future generations. I will call a meeting this week."

CHAPTER SEVEN: MAKING IT REAL

A hundred years after we are gone and forgotten, those who never heard of us will be living with the results of our actions.
— Oliver Wendell Homes, Supreme Court justice

The first six chapters of this book have dealt with the theoretical nature and methodology of the four master plans necessary for every intentional ministry. We began by talking about how most ministry leaders want "pretty pictures," a visual embodiment of a compelling ministry vision. The intention of my work here has been to convince you that the pretty pictures will be more realistic and will have a much better chance of coming to fruition if you are willing to take the leadership challenge of engaging in a thorough, intelligent, intentional, and honest master planning process. But there comes a time for pictures, imagery and drawings—and it is now! This is where the due diligence takes shape and an embodiment of the dreaming and planning take on a semblance of reality.

While I am a firm believer in all four master plans described in this book, I know that the physical representation of potential facilities is what most, if not all of you, were hoping to drill down into when you purchased this book. Given that, I am going to focus my attention to those aspects in this chapter.

Consider this the practical application of the first few chapters. The drawing phase of the facility master planning is both exciting and revealing. A lot of things will become evident to you and the project team once you have drawings in front of you. Is there adequate usable land for all of the desired building footprints, parking, buffers, vehicular aisles, storm water detention, athletic fields, and septic fields? If so, then praise the Lord! If not, then what? Can we buy more land? Can we modify our buildings to reduce the footprints by going vertical with multiple-story buildings? Should we relocate? Should we adjust our ministry programs to consider multiple services? You will find there are many challenges and questions to tackle.

You will also see if there will be any major issues with the topography that will either drive up the cost of the project or require an adjustment of the building structures or placement. Do we need to add retaining walls? How will storm water be addressed? Will a basement or lower level make good sense? Will the site need significant cut or fill of dirt? Will the sewage make use of gravity to flow or require a pump station? Will parking have to be tiered?

In addition to the insight it offers concerning site conditions, the drawing phase of the master plan is a tremendous tool for communicating vision. After all, isn't that why you wanted it for in the first place? The physical manifestation of the master plans will allow the church body to understand the direction the ministry leadership believes God is leading by actually "seeing" the vision that was established in chapter one.

I have offered a lot of details and processes in this book. Perhaps it would be helpful to see all of that applied in a real-life application. The following is a fairly straightforward case study of a church going through a master planning process.

Meet First Church. As described above, this church could be any congregation, even yours. Below are a few figures about the church:

Total Weekly Attendance: 760

Weekend Services: Three (they want to move to two)

Sale of Existing Facility: $4,200,000

Bought new land: $1,200,000

First Church plans to relocate to their new site and has been blessed to sell their former campus, which is no small feat. It generally takes three or more years to sell a church facility, so they've done well. They have bought a new site for $1,200,000 and their net cash on hand is $3,000,000. Many people in the church think that this net cash should be more than ample to build whatever they want for the new campus. They're right about $3,000,000 being a lot of money. But is it really enough?

After going through extensive visioning, target market study, and DNA analysis, they have determined that they would like to have a worship facility that will allow them to change their weekend worship program from three services to two services. With an average weekly attendance of 760, they would need to plan on a worship space that can seat about 800. Let's look at how we established that.

A good rule of thumb is that you design your new worship space for twice your current attendance. We assume that their current three services each has the same attendance, and when they change to two services, the attendance will be split equally as well. At an average weekly attendance of 760, each of the two new services will have 380 people in attendance before attendance grows. Using two times as the growth factor, we need to plan for just under 800 seats (two times the average per service). Most church growth experts will say that when you are at 80%capacity, you will feel full. Hoping that the ministry will grow by a factor of two in the new space, even a large sanctuary of 800 seats will start to feel full if attendance reaches 640 per service (total attendance in worship of 1,280 in the two services).

Stay with me as I take you on a rabbit trail for just a second. When you are considering the seating capacity of your worship space, the occupancy assumptions can drastically impact your planning.

Making it Real

I have been working with churches since the mid-1980s. During that era, most of the churches I served bought pews for their worship space. That was the norm, and the rule of thumb of 80% occupancy meant you were full. In a pew configuration, the code considers a seat to be every 18" in width. The middle seat on most airplanes is only 19 inches . . . pretty tight. A better measurement would be 21" to 22". So we have some space that the fire marshal says are seats that really aren't. But the other major factor with pews is the "spread out" space. You know, the place to lay my Bible, or a ladies purse or coat. Most people sitting in a pew take up far more than their allotted share of seating space, so the 80% rule was serious business and a key indicator for most churches.

In the 1990s and early 2000s, more and more churches moved to flexible seating . . . usually in the form of a stackable chair. These seats proved to be a great way to utilize a facility by having the flexibility to add or remove seating for other functions. Most of these seats were in the 20" to 22" range and even could interlock to give the illusion of a pew.

Two primary benefits for a church was the sheer cost (typically less than a pew) and the designated seat per person. It allowed for a quantifiable 1:1 ratio of people to chairs. This should have made the 80% rule obsolete, but there was still the mindset that we needed the "spread out" space and so many people still consumed two or more chairs to accommodate their personal property and desire for personal space. In addition, there was still a paradigm of allowing people to enter the worship space and sit wherever they liked. This meant that you would have spotty areas of seating with one chair here or two there or the entire front row empty. These two realities made the 80% rule still viable and necessary for worship space planning.

However, I think we are seeing a real trend that is impacting the change of the 80% rule. There are two primary contributors to this shift:

1. Theater-Style Seats: This has been a growing trend over the past decade and I believe it will likely continue. Theater seats allow you to have the 1:1 people to seat ratio, but most have an integral arm rest between seats so it is easier to obtain (and limit) personal space. In addition, the fold-down seat requires enough weight and force for it to fold that it is not as convenient for someone to try and use it to lay their Bible, as it will just fall to the ground, unless you have one of those large white leather coffee table Bibles.

   There are several other benefits that theater seats offer such as:

   • Allowing more seats in a similar space as chairs, in some cases 10-15% more seats. That gives you more bang for your buck

- Parking requirements will be "right-sized" compared to the calculations required for flexible seating (code says seven square feet per person in flexible seating)
- The same applies to your total restroom counts
- With the total number of occupants identified by the number of seats and not a square footage calculation, your HVAC system can also re right-sized, which can reduce costs both initially as well as related to life cycle

2. Crowd Control: Do you just let people sit wherever they like? Does your worship space fill up from the back to the front and from the aisles to the middle? I have seen a helpful trend being used by growing churches, what I will call "crowd control" or seat assigning. There are several attributes to this methodology that I see helping with your worship seating:

3. Segment off the worship space from front to back. I have seen many churches using pipe-and-drape or just ropes to barricade the back sections of the worship space until the front fills up and then will open up the back section in increments to keep the room full from front to back. This helps to ensure that the rooms fills before more seats are made available and also provides less distraction when

late-comers arrive as they can sit in the available seats in the rear.

4. Ushers direct traffic in the worship space. While this may sound controlling, what if your ushers helped people fill in every row from front to back and from aisle to aisle? Instead of letting people camp out on the end cap of a row, ask them to move all the way to the opposite end and then back-fill the row until it is 100% full. No saving seats. No spaces empty. While this may not feel natural, if you are space deprived—or feel like you are—and yet still have more seats than people, this will help you maximize the occupancy.

It is my opinion that if you utilize the above two methods to manage your worship seating, you can exceed the 80% rule to 85-90% . . . maybe more. You may ask why this is important to me (and to you). Here is why: It goes back to stewardship, financial and facility stewardship. If we can maximize the space God has already entrusted to us before we venture into another building initiative, we are being better stewards of our current spaces as well as the money entrusted to us.

Let's go back to our case study of First Church. Given the above assessment, First Church has determined that it needs a worship space of 800 seats. So how much net usable space will this require? Design professionals will use ratios ranging from 10 square feet per person to over

15 square feet per person as part of the planning process. Each of these is derived using varying criteria and assumptions. For this example, let's use 15 square feet per person, which should be adequate for the congregational seating (about 10 square feet per person), proportionally sized platform, and backstage space (baptismal, green room, and storage at about five square feet per person). The relevant equations show a need for about 12,000 square feet of net usable space.

First Church is a social church; the congregation likes to meet and greet both before and after services. They also want to have an area to interact with guests, information kiosks, and informational displays, all of which should be housed in a main gathering lobby. Because they plan to facilitate two services, First Church will also need a logical traffic pattern for the crowd to navigate the communal areas between the two services. The "turn" time between services can play a big role in the size of the lobby, commons, foyer, narthex, or other gathering space, as well as size and location of the parking structure and restrooms.

The most common ratio used by professionals for this space until recently was between one and two square feet per person. In the past, this space was intended to be used as a place to funnel people from the worship space to the outside or down a series of narrow corridors that led to the education, administration or fellowship areas. There was often a small table for tithing envelopes or general information along with 1-2 uncomfortable high-back chairs, usually not ones you would enjoy sitting in for any length of time nor were they arranged in a manner to encourage conversation or community.

For all practicality, the foyer was nothing more than a cattle chute, except for people. Not anymore.

That line of thinking has fortunately gone the way of the dodo-bird. Why? Because people want to connect. People want to do life together. We want to linger. We want to hangout. We want to do more than just pass through a space to merely get to the other side.

Given the above as well as many other cultural and practical influences, we are seeing these gathering spaces—what might be called the "commons"—be at least 50% the size of the worship seating with a preferred factor of 75-100% of the worship seating space. If we use 8-10 square feet per person for worship seating, that means we need to allocate 4-10 square feet per person in the common space vs. 1-2 square feet. In fact, one of the industry partners we collaborate with is trending their designs and concepts closer to 150%. That is a ton of space, and there are times that not all of it needs to be included in the "built environment" but can be captured in adjacent spaces outside the building and create an inside/outside commons that can be equally as effective and in many cases, be even more inviting.

In this instance, First Church intends to allow for 30

minutes between services, so the pressure on this space will be reduced some. In light of that, calculations based on five square feet per person are reasonable at a minimum, and yield a total of 4,000 square feet.

As part of the extensive discovery process, ministry leaders realized that they have need for onsite classrooms. This part of the evaluation can be more complex than just "x" seats per person in the worship space. In the case of education space, we have varying ages, learning styles, teaching styles, and activities. When we develop an education program, it will take a collaborative effort by various stakeholders over an extended period of time. For the sake of space, I am going to condense this programming to a simpler exercise.

I am going to use generalities based on the majority of the churches we assist. Obviously there are variations and exception. A widely accepted average ratio of children to adults is in the 22-24% range. The term "children" encompasses age zero through 5th grade as we are seeing most school districts promoting 6th graders to middle school. So, if we are planning 800 seats in worship, the number of children will likely be 176 – 192 per service. For ease of calculation, let's use 180.

To develop a high level assessment of the probable total amount of space for children, you can use a factor of 35 square feet per child. Again, there is far more complex assessments that must be made related to the age group and teaching style. For instance, in the crib baby area and "crawlers" we would suggest using 45-50 square feet per child due to furniture requirements and activity levels. However, if you have 5th graders seated in rows, you may be in the 12-15 square feet per child range.

For First Church, we are going to use the 180 children at 35 square feet for a total of 6,300 square feet. We would suggest adding 10-15% to that to accommodate toilet rooms in the classes, storage and resource areas, so let's bump that to 7,000 square feet (just a pinch over 10% factor).

Youth is the next age group. We see more and more ministries moving youth to an alternate time of the week in lieu of Sunday morning. While this clearly is not the same for every church, we are finding more churches in-cluding teens in the normal worship service experiences and not providing a separate Sunday morning education venue. With that said, there are still ample churches with a formal Sunday school program that is not simultaneous to their worship schedule. In those cases we find the need to provide dedicated space for the youth. So let's look at several variables. I am going to provide a couple youth scenarios:

<u>Youth Scenario 1:</u>

Premise: Youth do not meet separately on the week-end, but rather attend one of the regularly scheduled worship services. Youth activities are conducted at alternate times of the week and utilize space during those times that may have a different function on the weekend. In this scenario, there is little additional space that needs to be programmed or built. Youth can meet for large group worship and meetings in the worship center and use classrooms for break out groups.

There are a couple of considerations that must be factored in this approach. The first is a dedicated "pre-function" space. This may be a space that is a "hang-out" area with youth specific décor, game tables, couches, café, and the like. If that is a need, then assume you will need space to accommodate 20-25 square feet per youth. For the purpose of this example, let's assume that the youth comprise 6-8% of the total attendance of the church. If we are running 760, but intend to grow to 1200, we should plan on a youth population of 80-90. This equates to 1,600-2,250 square feet.

Youth Scenario 2:

Premise: Youth have a weekend educational session and need space for classrooms. We will use the same ratios and youth attendance factors as we did in Scenario 1, so we will plan on 80-90 youth. For the sake of this example, we will assume that 60% of the youth are middle school age (6th – 8th grade) and the balance is high school age (9th – 12th grade).

One successful way to plan for this space is to assume that you will need a common gatherings space, similar to that in Scenario 1, but with the possible inclusion of a "platform" area for a worship time in a large group setting. In addition, you would provide separate learning spaces for the different age groups, and possibly even break that down further into gender specific rooms. The amount of education space will be similar for each age group unless there is a difference in teaching/learning style philosophy. For the sake of this scenario, let's assume that these age groups will be sitting in rows, so we will use 15 square feet per youth (assume 90) for a total 1,350 Square feet for classroom space. When we couple that with the Scenario 1 allocation of space, we have a net total of 3,600 square feet.

In studying the church staff's collective DNA, it became clear that they enjoy working in a fairly close environment that encourages collaboration and interaction. They currently have what is considered an average of one pastoral staff person for every 100–150 people in the congregation, plus support staff. Given the current staffing, and figuring there will logically be growth, we determined that the church should plan for twelve workspaces (eight pastoral staff, assuming 1,200 people at 150 people per pastoral staff, and four support, assuming one support for every two pastoral staff) at an average size of 12 feet by 15 feet (180 square feet per work area). In addition, space would need to be planned for conference/meeting space, resource room, and work room. Based on the office/cubical needs, First Church would need another 2,160 square feet for the personnel and about 50% more space for the ancillary uses, for a total of 3,240 square Feet.

The above calculations are what are referred to as "net square footage." But we still need to take into account a "grossing factor." This factor includes electrical rooms, mechanical space, wall thickness, and other items. This can range from 10-25% depending on the type space and the stage of planning you are. For this example, we will use a factor of 25%. The way this is calculated is compiling your net square footage and multiplying it by 125% to realize the gross space that should be planned on. You will see the impact of this below.

There are obviously other spaces that various ministries will want to consider to meet their Ministry Master Plan and vision, such as recreation, adult education, small group meetings spaces, indoor play grounds, and other areas. But for this example, we will not take them into consideration. There are a number of other related costs and considerations, but for the sake of ink, let's look at the aspect of the Facility Master Plan that must be part of the equation . . . parking.

In the jurisdiction of First Church (and many others nationwide), the code requires a minimum 4:1 parking ratio. First Church has done their own parking analysis and has determined that they need a ratio of just 2 ¼:1.

With 800 seats, they will need 356 parking spaces. A typical stall (not including the handicap stalls) is 180 square feet, which translates to a need of 64,080 square feet for the parking spaces. As a rule of thumb, however, professionals suggest doubling that space in order to accommodate the drive aisles, turning radii, driveways, and other paved areas. This would increase the impervious conditions to 128,160 square feet, or about three acres of parking and pavement. As you can see, it takes a lot of land when you start including all the site improvements.

Here is a recap of the project square footage:

Worship space: 12,000 square feet

Commons: 4,000 square feet

Children: 7,000 square feet

Youth: 3,600 square feet

Administration: 3,240 square feet

Total net usable square footage: 29,840 square feet

Grossing factor: 1.25

Total square footage needed: 37,300 square feet. Don't miss this. Forgetting this factor will have significant impact on your functional space.

Now back to a key question: Do they have enough money to pay for this square footage? Can they afford it? Remember, they have $3,000,000 in cash. Surely, it is enough. You may be disappointed if you think it is. So what's next? I'll offer some closing thoughts in the next chapter.

CHAPTER EIGHT:
WHEN THINGS CHANGE

At this point you will have most of the data needed to make an informed decision about the next steps to take, including whether the best next step is to do nothing. There is no shame in stepping back and slowing the process. If you are not ready, the worst thing you can do is lead your church into an ill-advised project. At the same time, it can be almost as damaging to fail to proceed if you truly believe that the Lord is leading your ministry to reach your target and fulfill the passions He has given you. Don't squander this opportunity to further the work of the gospel and reach your community.

At the end of chapter seven I asked if First Church could afford the Facility Master Plan. I left the question a bit open-ended, but I want to drive home the importance of doing all four master plans. Some of the work of the plans can be done in conjunction with each other, but they are *all essential.* How can you plan the facilities without fully understanding the vision and mission of the church and how you intend to do ministry? You can't (or at least shouldn't) start to plan facilities without knowing your financial capabilities, and please make sure you are intentional with the Sustaining Master Plan. Do not be tempted to skip any one of these four planning exercises and don't just develop the plans, implement them. Few things pain me more than to see a church make plans but never implement them. If your intention is to just keep committees busy with planning without a deliberate desire to actually live out the plans, then let your congregation spend their time doing other things, like ministering to your community.

One last piece of encouragement for you as you reach what *appears* to be the conclusion of this initial phase of planning: resist the temptation to believe that the master planning processes are done. Don't allow all of your work to become useless and merely gather dust in a binder on a forgotten corner of your bookshelf.

Back in the first chapter of this book, I provided my definition of master planning. There were three components:

- A programmatic study of current and long-range ministry initiatives, and if/how facilities may or may not assist in accomplishing those plans.
- A vision of the future, beginning with today's realities.
- A clear and intentional big-picture view of the ministry's future based upon a ministry's needs, hopes, culture, DNA, and desires.

The word to remember about the process of master planning is "future." The word obviously has many connotations. One second from now is the future as is 100 years. Regardless of your reality of the future, it is not this instance. It I something yet to happen. And seeing that it has not happened yet, it is subject to variation, interpretation, and change.

Master plans are not a one-time document and initiative. They are living organisms that should be reviewed, revised, and renewed on a regular basis to reflect your current paradigm and your vision for the future. Depending on the growth of your church, change in leadership, community impacts, and other external factors, you may want to review the master plan every couple of years.

Things change. People change. Communities change. Methodologies change. And leaders learn from change. The age-old axiom is true: The only thing that is constant is change.

Change, in and of itself, does not require learning. But forward and positive change does require the skill of learning. Things are going to change. They can either change around you and you can ignore the change. Or we can learn and make adjustments to be part of an upward, positive, and sustainable change (until it is time to change again).

The fact is, change is inevitable. There is no escaping it. Change is a constant. All of this can affect the master plans and they may well need revising along the way. As you move forward with the master planning process, let me encourage you to follow these simple steps for change:

1. *Pray continuously*: I know this sounds obvious, but a facility initiative is not a task to be taken lightly. Both you and your team need to be in prayer about the project, the design, the finances, the impact to the community, and the church at large.

2. *Dream*: "What if?" Let you mind run wild. Think outside the box. If space and money were no object, what ministries would we start or expand?

3. *Plan thoroughly*: The first call to action in the planning stage is taking the dream and shaping realistic expectations related to dollars and space. As we explored earlier, this stage is where all of the money on the project is spent. The building phase is merely the fulfillment of the planning.

4. *Maintain realism*: This is easier said than done for most visionary leaders. It can be hard to pull in the dream when the proverbial rubber meets the road. Make sure your team has someone (internal or external) that can be the "budget cop" during the process, not to rain on the parade, but to keep reality squarely front and center.

5. *Draw pretty pictures!* This is the fun part. But be cautious: only draw what is realistic. Or at the very least, draw the dream but delineate the phases

based on the above realities. Nothing is more demoralizing to a congregation than to see a bunch of pretty pictures they cannot afford to build.

6. *Share the vision*: If you, as the leadership team, believe that this is a vision God has ordained and placed in your heart and mind, then by all means, share it . . . regularly. Now, you noticed that I did not say share the pretty pictures, although that is part of the vision. But the pretty pictures are not the vision. They are just the tool to help fulfill the vision. Do not get these mixed up, for you or your congregation.

7. *Repeat*: This is not a one and done process. Culture changes. Ministries change. Means and methods change. That means that the tools needed to do ministry will likely change as well. Be prepared to do some if not all of these master planning exercises on a regular basis. You will be glad you did.

You have done lots of work, and there is lots of work left to do as planning is a cycle and not a destination. This has been your heart's desire all along—God's work done in God's way, through your ministry. By intentionally focusing on the master planning processes, you can be confident that you have exercised both your faith and the facts with the wisdom God has given you to lead his people to kingdom heights. Plan on! Plan wisely.